They Called Me SKY HUNTER

MYRIAM HUSER

They Called Me Sky Hunter
Copyright © 2021 by Myriam Huser

All rights reserved. No part of this publication may be reproduced, distributed, or transmitted in any form or by any means, including photocopying, recording, or other electronic or mechanical methods, without the prior written permission of the author, except in the case of brief quotations embodied in critical reviews and certain other non-commercial uses permitted by copyright law.

Tellwell Talent
www.tellwell.ca

ISBN
978-0-2288-4761-8 (Hardcover)
978-0-2288-4760-1 (Paperback)
978-0-2288-4762-5 (eBook)

Joel

You were the initial spark of my incredible life.
Keep watching over me my guardian angel.

"You laugh at me because I'm different;
I laugh at you because you're all the same."
(Jonathan Davis)

"What doesn't kill you makes you stronger."
(Friedrich Nietzsche)

"Once men are caught up in an event, they cease to be afraid. Only the unknown frightens men."
(Antoine de Saint-Exupery)

"Perhaps He knew, as I did not, that the Earth was made round so that we would not see too far down the road."
(Karen Blixen)

CONTENTS

Preface ix
Back in the Sand Pit.. xi

PART ONE: NEVER QUIT 1

Switzerland, USA, Madagascar, Mozambique, South Africa, Denmark, Sweden, Morocco, Canada, Jordan, Iraq

Chapter 1   Learning Life 3
Chapter 2   America 10
Chapter 3   Pilot Is My Profession 19
Chapter 4   The Big Island 26
Chapter 5   White Girl 36
Chapter 6   Lost Between Three Continents............... 44
Chapter 7   Welcome to Canada!............................... 55
Chapter 8   The Beautiful Rockies 63
Chapter 9   Spiral Over Baghdad............................... 70
Chapter 10 Can I Have a Refund?............................. 83

PART TWO: THE DREAM IS ALIVE.......................... 87

Chad, Sudan, France, Algeria, Uganda, Tanzania, Ethiopia, Canada

Chapter 11 Africa, Here I Come 89
Chapter 12 Surgery 100
Chapter 13 Rebels Attack 107
Chapter 14 Moving On 116
Chapter 15 How Many Guns?................................. 119

Chapter 16	Horror and Beauty	128
Chapter 17	Detained	147
Chapter 18	Time to Go	162
Chapter 19	Sahara	171
Chapter 20	Red Earth	183
Chapter 21	My *Out of Africa*	187
Chapter 22	Kilimanjaro	197
Chapter 23	Ethiopia	208
Chapter 24	New Job, New Life	221
Chapter 25	Ferry Flight	224
Chapter 26	Sleeping with Bears	235
Chapter 27	Baptized by Fire	241

Conclusion 249
Acknowledgements 253

PREFACE

Pursuing a dream takes all you have to reach it. But it doesn't stop there. Once you reach a goal it takes even more to keep it alive. With many ups and downs, my life so far has been a great adventure that continues to this day. Full throttle, here's the story that shaped who I am.

Respecting the privacy of people who have crossed my path, I've changed names to protect identities.

An ordinary life turned into an extraordinary life!

My happy place

BACK IN THE SAND PIT

It's 5:00 a.m. The sound of a car engine wakes me up. All curled up under a pile of four blankets, I'm still shivering. It's so cold—barely 10°C—but it's time to get up. It's December 2015, and I'm in Niger in the middle of the Sahara. My room is a container with no heater. A single bed, a tiny metal table and a chair are all there is. I share a bathroom with a colleague whose room is on the other end of the container. We are a contingent of ten people living in this remote camp in the middle of the desert.

After a quick breakfast and coffee, I was sitting in the cockpit an hour later as daylight appeared on the horizon. It was time to start this first long day and get airborne. I was still wearing my jacket over my flight suit, and my hands were freezing. It was winter in the desert after all, and even if the days were getting warmer, temperatures dropped to near freezing overnight.

With the engines running, the sweet sound of turbines put a smile on my face. A few minutes more to get the equipment up and running, and once the technician sitting in the back of the cabin gave the "OK to go," we started rolling down the runway for departure position. A quick call to our flight follower in the dispatch room on the other side of the planet in the United States let him know we were ready to start. He would follow us live, and we'd be in contact every thirty minutes to confirm that operations were normal. He would instantly know if anything out of the ordinary happened and dispatch a rescue team immediately.

Setting the power for take-off, I had to remember that it would feel different from what I was used to. We were much heavier than normal, so I needed to compensate. A regular Twin Otter was limited to 12,500 lb., but with the special type rating I received, I was now flying with 14,000 lb. on survey and over 16,000 lb. on ferry flights. Most of the additional weight was fuel. With the extra fuel tank installed in the baggage compartment, we could remain airborne up to six hours. For our routine, however, we would be flying five hours in the morning and, after a quick lunch break, up again for another four hours in the afternoon. Needless to say, having to maintain full concentration flying manually and having to hold a line within a few metres off to the right or left and up and down, we were lucky to have two pilots on-board to share the work. No autopilot was allowed on survey mode.

My lead captain took the controls first and showed me how it was done. It was still early morning, the air was smooth and calm, so it was the best time for my first trial. Survey work consists of flying over a predetermined land area, criss-crossing it as if you wanted to draw an imaginary chess board. While doing so, different instrumentations on-board are recording data to create a geophysical map of what lays underground to be used for future oil and mineral exploration. Our aircraft was fitted with Lidar, Full Tensor Gravity Gradiometer and other systems.

Once Captain Jim finished the first line, he proceeded with a tight turn and again explained how to do it efficiently to save time. He then handed over the controls and, with my eyes locked on the bar indicating my position, I tried to maintain a perfect track to keep us on the survey line. Having previous experience flying this type of aircraft definitely helped, and it was the reason why the company hired me. The plane just became an extension of my body as I sensed what was happening and reacted automatically. While I was allowed to stay within twenty-five metres of the centreline, I aimed to keep it within five to ten.

I had always been a perfectionist, and challenging myself to do better was the way I functioned in everyday life. It amazed me how much concentration it took to remain focused for so long. It was like flying a precision approach but, instead of doing it for just a few minutes, it had to be maintained for up to an hour and a half while flying over a hundred-kilometre line at a time. The funny thing was, as soon as someone talked and expected me to answer, I was thrown off-line and had to struggle to regain control and remain within limits. But that's what was required. I was told this was normal at first, and it would get easier with experience. Soon, I'd be able to relax and listen to music. The cool part of this job.

I had left home on Christmas Eve, which was just perfect as I didn't have a reason to celebrate the holiday season. With no kids, single and living alone after too many failed relationships, I was happy to work during that time of year. After a simple holiday dinner, my brother dropped me off at Vancouver Airport where the long journey to Niger began. The first leg, overnight, took me to Montreal where I arrived at six in the morning. With a long Christmas Day layover, I finally boarded the next flight that took me from Montreal to Paris. With six hours to wait again between flights, I walked around Charles de Gaulle and enjoyed a breakfast I've always loved in this country: coffee and fresh croissants. Can't beat French pastry! It had been a few years since my previous visit, having settled on the south coast along Côte d'Azur. I miss Provence sometimes, it's such a beautiful part of France.

When I finally arrived in Niger, the sounds and smells of Africa—the same feelings that arose every time I set foot on this continent, no matter which country—greeted me as I left the airport. Somehow, I had a feeling of being "home" even though this wasn't where I grew up.

The next morning, I boarded a small charter plane loaded with my luggage and as much cargo as possible—mainly food and bottles of water, the only way to re-supply the camp with necessities—to take me to my crew and what would be my home for the next couple of months. As we started rolling down the runway for take-off, I looked out the window and was reminded of a neighbouring country where I had lived and experienced so much ten years earlier.

When I finally arrived in Agadem, I realized why management were a little hesitant to send me there. Living conditions were at bare minimum; there's not much comfort for a lady out there. There was only a Chinese oil and gas camp, an airstrip to commute workers in and out for rotation, a Niger military detachment for security and our camp there. I was glad they had changed their minds once I explained I am very familiar with living in harsh conditions and being the only female on a team. Sand surrounded us for miles and miles. I'd been in camps like this before, but never in such a small one; it was just large enough to enclose the ten containers needed for our sleeping quarters, kitchen, mess and office. For security reasons, we were not allowed to step outside the barbwire fence. Even for the short five-minute trip between the airstrip and the camp we had to be escorted by armed military pickup trucks. Boko Haram was attacking villages, killing security forces and kidnapping civilians daily not too far to the south and east, so the camp took our security seriously.

Those tight security rules sounded a little over the top considering I'd be criss-crossing this vast land daily in a slow aircraft at very low altitude for the purpose of surveying. We couldn't be an easier target for rebel groups in the area. But regardless, I was thrilled and excited about this new job. As soon as I entered the camp, I was greeted by the team: the two other pilots, our engineer who ensured the plane was airworthy every day, a medic who assured we were as well, our security consultant who advised of any security threats, and the geophysical technician crew. They all made me feel comfortable right away and did everything possible to help me fit it. Jim advised me to take time to settle in, then we could meet in the mess to review details and prepare for work.

"See you in five minutes!" I said.

He smiled.

That's all the time I needed to store my luggage in the container and refresh a bit. Then the orientation began. He explained how we worked on survey flights and gave me tips on how to use the special instruments for best results. Then he told me I had better learn quickly because he needed to sign me off as captain before the end of the week. Another new pilot was due to arrive at that time who not only had no experience in survey but also no experience on the Twin Otter. I basically needed to get up to speed quickly so I could assume the role of lead pilot when Jim left for his break. No pressure! I loved challenges, especially this type, though I was a little nervous because being precise enough for this type of work is something you either have or you don't. I was determined to try my best and would know soon enough if I was cut out for it.

Transmitting on radio and outside communication was not allowed while on survey due to the geophysical recording system. Only the intercom would not interfere. We were all focused on doing our own work, and the best way to make those long hours pass by quickly was to listen to some good tunes. So, with my hands starting to cramp and my shoulders and upper body tensing up trying to make this work, next to me I saw Captain Jim jamming along with music in his ears, trying to make me lose concentration and screw it up.

"Naaah, you're not going to get to me!" I said, and we had a good laugh.

By afternoon, I was feeling good, and when Jim said, "Are you sure you've never done this before?" I relaxed and realized I was actually doing well for a newbie.

By the end of the day, I was feeling tired, still jet-lagged from my long journey to Africa and a full day of constant concentration. Once back at camp, I relaxed for an hour, trying not to fall asleep before supper that was served at six. When the cook called everyone, we gathered in the mess container, which was lightly decorated for the holiday season, the only reminder that we'd be celebrating New Years in just a few days.

The food was good, and our plates were filled with more than we could eat. There were fresh apples and bananas on a tray, and I was advised to enjoy them quickly. They had arrived on my transit flight from the capital and, as these flights occurred only every few weeks for crew change, fresh fruits and vegetables didn't last long. I quickly understood that our meals would normally consist of canned food, mostly green beans served with pasta or rice. There was also meat kept in a freezer, but as I didn't—or should I say, couldn't—eat red meat, the meals would quickly become boring and simple.

The third day was my day off because the three pilots rotated two days on followed by a day off. This basically meant being bored out of my mind sitting in my container or walking around the camp like an inmate in a prison yard. A sudden and horrible cry interrupted my planned sleep-in, and I jumped out of bed to look outside.

"What's going on out there?" I asked one of my campmates who was walking by.

"Oh yes, we forgot to tell you. The locals slaughter a goat every morning right outside our camp on that sand dune," he said.

Just what I need to hear this early in the morning, I thought.

Well, I was up now. I grabbed a cup of coffee and the book I had started and found a place to sit in the sun. It was much warmer outdoors than in my container, and it was going to take a few hours before the heat outside started to warm the inside. The idea of keeping the doors open to make this occur faster was not really an option, as you would just end up with your room full of flies or sand.

Speaking of sand, the sky was turning from blue to orange, and I had a feeling a storm was on the way. It was the beginning of sandstorm season after all. I had learned to read the signs a few years back in a similar environment. At lunchtime, my feeling was confirmed as the wind started picking up and more sand lifted into the air. Unfortunately, this meant no flights for us. Flying so close to the ground to survey was simply a no-go as we would have had zero visibility. Luckily, this lasted only a few hours and, with calm wind again, the sand had time to settle down overnight.

The next morning, I was back in the cockpit. On my fourth day flying survey, I was signed off officially as captain for the company and was having the time of my life. Call me crazy, but that's the way it was. Where some people probably find fun in a nightclub, I found excitement working under conditions most would likely forgo.

At the beginning of my second week, the new pilot arrived, and Jim was counting on me to help teach him everything he needed to know. That was going to have to wait, however, because a sandstorm arose overnight and we were hiding in our rooms. The wind was blowing so hard that it was vibrating the container walls. Sand was creeping inside through the gaps around the window and the door, filling the air with a light dust and making breathing uncomfortable. The air pressure was such that I literally had trouble breathing, feeling as if I was suffocating. Tired of constantly sweeping the sand, I needed to plug all the holes to make my container as airtight as possible. First I rolled a bath towel and tucked it along the bottom of the door. Then I pulled some of the stuffing from my extra pillow and pushed it inside the sliding metal rack of the window. I knew I wouldn't ever open that window anyway, so I blocked every opening. Duct tape to hold all of this in place and, voila, I now had a sand-proofed container.

The storm went on for five days without a break. Everyone in the camp was getting frustrated as no work could be done while the survey was on hold. Eventually, we didn't know what do to with ourselves anymore. Reading a book, watching a movie on the computer, doing jumping jacks and abdominal exercises on the floor, reading some more, staring at the ceiling while listening to music—the days were long. Highlights were mainly lunch and supper as they provided a chance to get out of our container. Though nobody had much to say, we ate our plate of pasta and beans, or rice and beans, and wondered when the storm would end.

When it finally stopped, we had to wait an extra day for the dust to settle before visibility was good enough to get airborne. Then we tossed a coin to determine the unlucky one who wasn't going to fly that day. I was so looking forward to getting back in the air and actually doing something with my days. If anymore of these sandstorms occurred, it would be a very long rotation of work and a very slow process to get it done.

I needed to find ways to stay fit and maintain a healthy mind through exercise. The men worked-out by flipping a huge tire they called the "big bastard" (they painted the name on it). But, for a relatively small woman, it was so heavy that I couldn't lift it off the ground without straining my back. So, after speaking with the security officer, I obtained approval to run outside along the fence of the camp, which became my routine every evening. I ran in circles, but at least I was moving. It was difficult running on unstable sand, and it looked more like I was wobbling than actually jogging. After an hour of this, I was sweating and full of sand, but I felt much better.

The weeks passed, and the flying was going well with a mix of sandy days and great visibility that revealed amazing details in the desert. One of them was the memorial of the UTA Flight 772. On September 19, 1989, the DC-10 aircraft had taken off from N'Djamena, Chad, and an explosion blew the plane up over the Sahara Desert less than an hour later. The memorial built in 2007 was made of black rock and had the shape and size of the DC-10 within a compass. They used the remains of one wing as a compass point. It was partially covered with sand, probably due to the last storm, but the sight of it was very touching. It instantly brought back memories of someone close to me who I had lost some twenty years ago from a plane crash in the desert.

Joel, the first love of my life, was a pilot. I was nineteen when I met him and just finishing my apprenticeship as a travel agent. He was flying for a local company in Switzerland when we met on a business trip. He was also doing contract work for a humanitarian cause in Western Sahara during that time, where his life ended tragically. It was probably why I felt at home every time I flew over the Sahara. A sense of belonging.

It had been over five weeks since I arrived, and most of the crew were changing shifts with their back-to-back crew arriving to replace them. I originally agreed to do an extra-long rotation so I'd have another three weeks to go before I saw civilisation again. Jim was going on a well-deserved vacation in about a week. Every evening for the next few days, he showed me the paperwork side of his job so I could take over while he was gone. No other crew member would replace him. The two remaining members, the other new pilot and I, were to assume his duties.

The hard work and difficult living conditions wore me out quickly, but the technical part of this job was motivating. And we were such a great team, we always found a way to laugh at our situation and make the day go by in a fun way.

A week later, I enjoyed my last day-off getting extra sleep, doing laundry and reading another book. I wouldn't have much time to relax until the end of my rotation. For the next ten days, I'd be flying non-stop unless a new sandstorm hit. The following morning, I said goodbye to Jim as he waited for his ride back to the capital. Then I got on with my flight for the day.

The weather was beautiful, and I crossed my fingers that it would remain so for a while to finish the job quickly. With only a few thousand more kilometres to survey, we hoped to finish before our relief crew arrived.

Day four of this "no rest days" stretch arrived with good visibility, as it had for the past ten days or so. But because we were still in the middle of sandstorm season, we knew this couldn't last. By the end of the morning, the wind started picking up, though visibility was still crystal clear, so we kept going. It was getting rough and, being so close to the ground with such wind, turbulence was strong. On the northwest side of the survey block, we encountered up to sixty-knot crosswinds. Crazy! To maintain the line, I flew sideways and, instead of looking through the front windshield to see where I was going, I resorted to looking out the side window.

It was odd because there was still no sand swirling off the ground, and the technician didn't call off the flight either. When the turbulence got too strong, the data collected was usually rejected, meaning we had to fly those lines over again on a better day. Once I reached the end of my line, after fighting hard to keep within limits despite the very strong turbulence, I asked: "Do you think this will pass?"

Our tech answered: "Probably not!"

"What? And you let us work so hard for over an hour without saying anything?" I replied.

Laughing, he replied: "I just wanted to see if you could maintain it!"

The co-pilot and I looked at each other, shook our heads and joined in the laughter with him. Well, that was fun!

After lunch, visibility was still holding up and the winds were weaker on the other side of the block, so we decided to go toward that sector to continue working. Flying over a desert might sound boring, but the patterns, tones and colours are constantly changing. When the sun is getting low on the horizon, vivid oranges contrast with the shadows playing against the dunes. It's simply mesmerising.

BACK IN THE SAND PIT

I was dead tired that evening and nearly fell asleep at the dinner table with my head in my green beans. The doctor was a bit concerned and wondered if I was fit enough to keep flying at this pace. But all I really needed was a good night's sleep. After supper I said goodnight and hit the sack by seven o'clock.

The wind died down during the night, and we were able to resume work the next morning. Having slept ten hours straight, I was feeling pretty good and ready for another long day. Back in the air, again around mid-morning, the winds picked up. However, something was different this time. Within a few minutes, the temperature dropped. Sticking my fingers out the window, I could feel it getting cold. Not a good sign. Also, the wind shifted and was now coming from the east. Having flown in the Algerian Desert a few years back, I remembered these were two sure signs of a coming sandstorm. We were flying in an area to the east of our camp, approximately forty-five minutes away, so I advised the crew to be vigilant. As soon as we saw sand lifting off the ground, it was time to turn around and head home. My suspicions were confirmed within the next thirty minutes when we suddenly saw the first few patches of dust rise between dunes and quickly filling the sky in front of us.

"Time to break the line and head back," I said over the intercom.

We climbed, set maximum power and selected the "direct to" mode on the GPS which gave us a heading straight back to destination, and called dispatch to let them know we were on our way back. Approximately ten miles from the airstrip we began to worry because we couldn't see the ground anymore. We might have to fly an extra hour to make it to the only alternate airport in the area that would allow us to land using standard instrument approach. But then we came out of a dusty cloud and saw the runway and our camp right in front of us. I quickly prepared the plane for landing, bringing the power levers back, the propellers full forward, and lowering the flaps to slow down and reach the targeted speed for safe landing. We touched down with the wind blowing debris around us, and we had just enough time to shut down the engines and close the doors before being engulfed in thick sand. I couldn't see more than ten metres ahead. That was close!

So that was it for that day and, for the first time, I wasn't complaining about having to stay hidden in my container all afternoon. I slept while the wind howled outside blocking out any noise that could wake me.

Interestingly enough, the sandstorm lasted only overnight, and the next morning it was clear and time to go again. By six we were airborne and watching a magnificent sunrise over the sandy horizon. However, soon enough the strong winds returned, and within a couple of hours the saga repeated itself. But today it moved in faster. By the time we arrived over the camp airstrip the wind was already blowing strong, but we had to give it a try before deciding to divert. Luckily, the wind blew straight down the runway, making it easier to land. Knowing that there was nothing around we could hit, I made my final turn a few miles out from the runway threshold, lined up precisely using GPS and slowly approached hoping the runway would soon appear for a normal landing right in front of us.

The frustrating part of a sandstorm was that, while you might see the ground right below you, forward visibility could be close to zero, and it feels like you're hitting a wall. Fortunately, the Twin Otter is a relatively slow plane and our runway was long enough. So even if I only saw the runway once over it, I had plenty of time and space to land. And that's exactly what happened. With over forty knots of headwind, we came over the runway, rocking as if we were in a washing machine tumbler. I was fighting against the wind gusts to keep my wings level and tried to bring the plane down on the runway as smoothly as I could. Once the main landing gear touched down, I quickly pushed the nose down to bring the nose wheel on the ground to counteract the wind trying to lift us back in the air, and I pulled the power levers into reverse. We basically stopped within twenty metres. *God, I love this airplane*, I thought. *It is such an amazing workhorse!* The co-pilot looked at me with amazement.

"That's what a few thousand hours flying this aircraft does for you," I said with a smile.

The storm didn't let up over the following two days, so we held off again and were stuck sitting around for hours. I was disappointed because we could have finished the project within these few days just before the crew leader returned. But that wasn't going to happen, and two days dragged on like they'd never end. The excitement of going home made this wait unbearable. Now I was only hoping the sandstorm would stop in time so the charter flight bringing in the new crew and taking me out to catch my international flight would make it on schedule.

Luckily, on Friday morning the winds stopped. But visibility was still very poor. A few hours on stand-by while the charter flight was delayed tested my patience that day, but they finally arrived to pick me up, and I was about to start my journey back home for a well-deserved rest. After a quick handover with the crew leader, I said goodbye to everyone and headed down to the airstrip one last time. I knew I wouldn't be returning to this base, as they would be finishing the project before my next rotation. With passengers and luggage on-board, the plane was back in the air and we were on our way to Niamey, Niger, by mid-afternoon. With a smile on my face, I closed my eyes and reflected on an amazing life and the long road that had brought me to this moment.

Short break while refuelling during survey missions in Niger, 2015

The DHC-6 fitting with survey tail boom and the air-conditioning system that is plugged in at all times while on the ground at the end of the day mission.

PART ONE

NEVER QUIT

CHAPTER 1

LEARNING LIFE

It all began with a teenage dream. 1986, I was thirteen, definitely a tomboy, and was already feeling out of place compared to the other girls at school. My bedroom was plastered with posters, but they weren't images of actors or singers. No, I had posters of F-14 Tomcats instead. The aviation virus was already running wild in my blood; all I could think of was flying.

Born in a small village in the middle of the magnificent Swiss Alps, my childhood in the 70s and 80s was spent between school, playing outdoors (we didn't have much on TV), being harassed by a brother a year older than I, and doing my chores. I enjoyed reading as well, and we had a collection of encyclopedias describing different countries all around the world and detailing the cultures, geography and history. They were filled with photos, and I loved flipping through the pages, dreaming of far away lands. Africa was particularly fascinating! The vastness filled with incredible wildlife and that sense of freedom was calling me. It's around that time that the movie *Out of Africa* came out. It wasn't so much the love story that had me, but the scenery, that incredible landscape, rich in colour and open spaces. I knew I had to see it for myself some day.

My father was a salesman, and my mother stayed at home with us until I was a teenager. It was mostly just the four of us, and we rarely had contact with the extended families on both sides who were living in different parts of the country. My father was from the Italian part of Switzerland, my mother from the German part, and I grew up in the French part where they had settled after they married.

Every summer we would go on a camping trip either in France or Spain to enjoy a few weeks of fun at the beach. The rest of the year we mainly just went to school and played at home. The outdoors was always a big part of our lives. We skied every winter, hiked those same mountains in the summer and roamed the forests foraging for mushrooms or different flowers and berries to make jelly and beverages.

My fascination with military aircraft probably came from the day I visited the aircraft carrier USS *Saratoga* (CV-60). I was ten years old and on vacation in Spain with my family when we had an opportunity to board the aircraft carrier and explore it for a day while it was in the Mediterranean. The floating complex was incredible to see, but the aircraft lined up on the deck triggered something within me I can't explain. From that day, every time a plane passed over our house, I stared at the sky to look at it. I wanted to be up there, and somehow I knew it was where I belonged.

One day at school when I was twelve, we had to write down what we would like to do when we grew up. We could choose from a list, and my first choice was pilot, of course. But the teacher returned the sheet to me and said: "You can't choose pilot! You are a girl, and this is only for the boys." My parents had other ideas for my future anyway. They had decided I would start by doing the apprenticeship at a travel agency after I finished secondary school. Once I was old enough, they had me apply with Swissair to become a stewardess. I can still remember clearly when they made me dress up as a "lady" and took pictures of me in our garden. The photos were requested by the airline for the application. When I received a rejection a few weeks later because I was too short (in those days, the minimum height was 175 cm), I was probably the happiest girl in the world!

For the time being, I kept my dream tucked away in my heart and would not talk about it with anymore. I was thirteen years old when the *Challenger* disaster occurred and can remember being touched by it. I cut out every newspaper article I could find about this NASA disaster.

Even though I had a happy childhood, my brother and I grew up in a very strict family, my parents being very authoritarian. As teenagers it went from bad to worse when we were starting to want more than to just stay at home after school. The fun and outgoing little girl I once was transformed into a very shy and introverted young woman. Unable to join my school friends at parties and outings, I was left aside more and more as if I didn't belong to the group anymore, and the transition from school to the active workforce at the travel agency at seventeen years old was a tough time for me. Forced into doing something I wasn't comfortable with, I couldn't even argue my way out onto something else as the response was always: "We have enough problems with your brother."

He was on an electrician apprenticeship and was really good at that, but it was always the school part that was the trouble because he often failed his exams; it became a great concern. As always, he was the priority, so I had to lay low and just be the good girl.

Within the last couple of years of my apprenticeship, dealing with too much drama at home apparently wasn't enough. Just when I thought it couldn't get any worse, I had to cope with sad and dramatic events that would teach me how cruel life can be.

It started with the death of a childhood friend who had already gone through many difficulties at the age of seventeen. One morning, I received a phone call telling me that she had killed herself the night before. After school, she had taken a bus to a place selected in preparation for her plan, dropped off her backpack with a goodbye letter and jumped off a cliff. I blamed myself for a long time for not having seen it coming. That same morning, as every morning before, we had sat side by side on the bus and talked as though it was a normal day. We were both feeling a bit like outcasts compared to the other girls who enjoyed freedom and lived fun teenage lives. Her suicide was a shock, and I just couldn't understand it.

A few months later, my family completely broke apart after my brother had a terrible car accident with his girlfriend and her sister on-board. They were on their way home from Italy where they had spent their vacation. To maximise their time there, my brother had decided to enjoy their last day at the beach, and they got on the road in the evening. They drove all night to make it back in time for our father's birthday because our parents had insisted we both be home for it. With the girls sleeping and nobody keeping up conversation to keep him awake, he fell asleep while on the highway. They were lucky to survive the crash, but they sustained severe injuries and were hospitalized for a long time. My brother's girlfriend never walked again.

My brother wanted to leave the hospital he was in to go visit his girlfriend in another one hours away, but my parents disapproved of their relationship. The constant fighting at home, as they refused to accept that we were adults, brought the tension unbearably high. They couldn't control everything anymore and, as soon as my brother celebrated his twentieth birthday, he packed a bag and left home without looking back. I was nineteen, and even though I wished I could have done the same, I had a few more months to go before finishing my apprenticeship. Being naïve, I also was too afraid to follow in his footsteps, so I stayed home. Now, not only did I have to experience the usual drama, I was also getting an earful of my parents' anger about my brother's departure. Many years later, he said that if he had known better at the time, he would have taken me with him. But, in hindsight, how could he? He had nothing and was struggling to find the means to start his own life.

At the beginning of the following year, I was preparing for final exams for my travel agent diploma and feeling happy because I could see some light at the end of the tunnel. I had already planned to leave my home country after I finished my contract at the agency to become an au pair with a family in California for a year. I was going there to learn English and experience what life had to offer away from home.

It was also a time when I finally experienced the joy of having a boyfriend. I met Joel, a pilot, during a work trip while visiting hotels and restaurants on the island of Corsica. From that day on, we spent as much time together as we could. He took me with him on some of his flights when he had an empty seat, which got me more and more fascinated with aviation.

When I trusted him enough to tell him of my dream of becoming a pilot, he was so positive and encouraged me to pursue my goals.

He said that there's no good reason why I shouldn't be able to. My eyes were wide open and a huge smile lighted my face when I realized that anything is possible if I really wanted it. His support meant a lot.

While we were discussing my dream, he removed a necklace he was wearing that had a beautiful little airplane on it. Asking me to turn around, he put it on me and said while laughing, "You'll give it back to me the day we divorce." Feeling loved and respected made me feel good about myself. It helped me regain my confidence about the person I was and wanted to be, and for once, instead of being judged and criticized, someone was pushing me in a positive way.

Ten days before my final exam, he had to leave for the Western Sahara where he was contracted to fly for the United Nations (UN). On June 22, I woke up happy and excited knowing that this day was my final test and studies would end. No more school, just another month and a half at the office and it would be over. I was feeling relaxed and confident while sitting on the bus on my way to the train station. The bus was running late, so I had to hurry not to miss my train ride. As I was getting out of the bus and rushing for the pier, I caught a glimpse of the headline on the newspapers at the kiosk. One of them said, "Humanitarian pilot dead in Mauritania."

For the next fifteen minutes, I felt like something was wrong. I kept telling myself Joel was in Western Sahara, not Mauritania. Where is Mauritania anyway? Not to worry. I got off the train and walked to school as planned with my best friend Caroline for our last oral exam. But I had to put my mind at ease first, so I bought a newspaper to read the full article and stop worrying for nothing. As I read, I looked at Caroline, looked back at the article and read the name of the pilot. *No, it's not possible!* The paper fell to the ground. Joel was dead! He was gone. My love would never come back from the desert. The rest of that day is a big blur, but I remember having to postpone my test. I visited Joel's parents' house and met them for the first time.

I took the German oral exam the next day. The teachers were as sensitive as possible with my grief and this weakened person before them. I remember the funeral, putting my hand on his coffin and feeling a strange energy surging through my hand.

My time with Joel had been brief as our relationship lasted only a few short months. But he had come into my life at a critical time, when I was the most vulnerable and only starting to understand what life is about. The love and respect he gave me in such a short time is something I have not experienced since.

There was more drama at home too. A few days later, when my brother came to visit and to pick up some of his belongings, a fight ensued between him and my father that ended their relationship once and for all. I left the house and wandered into the street in a daze. *Why can't it all go away?* I thought. I wanted to get away from all of this insanity, I wanted Joel to return and take me with him. Eventually, a concerned neighbour picked me up on the road and brought me back home where I was given something to sleep. I cried every night for days, weeks. The sad reality of life had hit me in the face like a brick.

CHAPTER 2

AMERICA

December 1, 1993, finally arrived—the beginning of a new chapter. I was about to leave my family life behind and start a new one. At least, that's the way I looked at it. I was more than ready to get away from all the darkness filling up my days. I was flying across the ocean all the way to the west coast of the US where a family of six was awaiting my arrival. I would spend the next year in Visalia, CA, primarily to learn English.

But I also had another secret goal in mind.

I settled into my new home quickly and got to know my new family. There was Tim, the dad, whom I would only see on evenings and weekends because he worked a lot. Monica, the mom, worked partly with him and would leave in the morning and return by mid-afternoon. She would bring the twelve-year-old twin boys, Jarod and Shane, home from school. Then there were the two girls, Lacy and Jordana, nine and six, who I would mainly care for during the day.

I had the mornings to myself, so I attended an English class at the local college for the first four months. I would exercise at the local gym after class a couple of days a week, otherwise I just stayed at home with my daily routine of cleaning up and doing laundry. I had plenty to do living in a big house on a ranch with four kids and two busy parents. At lunchtime, I'd pick up the girls at school and prepare their meals. Lacy would then return to school and Jordana would take her nap. Then I had a break and usually watched TV as a way to improve my English. Even if I didn't understand all of it, putting the words I'd hear into the context of what I was seeing did the trick. Together with my classes, the TV and conversing with the kids, I quickly learned the language.

Since my weekends were usually free, I decided to begin my "secret project" a month after arriving. I talked to Monica about taking flying lessons, and she loved the idea and encouraged me. She looked into the different options I had in the area and put me in contact with an instructor who owned his own airplane at a small airfield not too far from our house. She made me an appointment for an orientation flight, and as simple as that I was in the air, sitting on the left seat of a C172 getting my first taste of flying. I was thrilled and hooked.

And so it all started. I planned to take a flight lesson every weekend and, for the theory part, bought study books and the famous King video. Everyone in aviation remembers John and Martha King. They made video tapes with all the lessons needed to learn how to fly an airplane. So here I was, with my limited English, taking flying lessons. At first, I couldn't understand much of what the instructor, Gary, was saying. But I didn't care. I was flying! He was a great guy and had a lot of patience. He motivated me and was determined to help me as much as possible. At the beginning, it was a very slow and intense process to review the lesson of the week because I had to basically translate words using my dictionary to gain understanding, one sentence at a time. But I progressed well in learning English and, soon enough, I was able to maintain a conversation and understand most of it.

One of my most unforgettable experiences was my first solo, which occurred rather quickly since I had only logged about ten instructional hours. One day as I was about to finish my flight lesson with Gary, we returned to the field and landed. As we started to taxi back to the hangar to park the plane, Gary said, "Turn back for another take-off." He told me I was ready and could now do three take-offs and landings on my own. He said he would be standing on the edge of the runway watching me and that everything would be fine. Then he opened his door and stepped out! Without thinking much, I positioned myself, applied power and took off. The wheels lifted off the ground, and I climbed for my first solo traffic pattern. Only then did I look toward the right seat and finally realize nobody was there. I thought, *Oh my God! I'm alone! OK, OK, everything is fine. I can do this. I have to do this now. I have to fly and land this plane because there's nobody here to help me.*

The anxiety lasted for a split-second and a huge grin replaced it. I felt the adrenaline rush through my body. I was so happy and proud. I thought of Joel and said, "Look, I'm doing it!" As the plane turned, I prepared for landing and made a smooth touch down. I taxied back to the head of the runway and did it two more times. Once I was finished, I taxied to the hangar and shut down the engine. As I stepped down from the cockpit, Gary congratulated me—with a pair of scissors! They were for the ritual of cutting off a piece of the student's shirt worn during the first solo. Then he wrote the name, date and the event on it as a souvenir. I was glad I hadn't worn my favourite shirt that day!

I was constantly busy with flying lessons, collecting the kids from school, feeding their horses and cleaning the kids' rooms and the rest of the house. But I truly enjoyed every day there. When the family went on a ski holiday to the mountains and on a trip to the beaches of Santa Barbara, I went with them and had fun.

I was experiencing life on my own, and I loved it even more when the time came to begin solo cross-country flights. At first, I was nervous. I had to fly through busy airspace to find airports I'd never been to before. But the stress quickly turned into an amazing feeling of freedom. I loved being up there; something magical happened every time I became airborne. As soon as the wheels lifted off the ground, I suddenly forgot everything happening on Earth. All the worries would disappear, replaced with a feeling of total peace.

In the second half of my year there, the family moved to an extended mobile home they rented on a large ranch site while they were having their home relocated. I loved it! I was surrounded by horses, cattle and cowboys all day long. There was a huge pool normally used for injured horses, but the kids and I used it the most. In the evening, I would join the cowboys in the barn and play cards while listening to them play guitar and sing. For a girl who grew up in the Swiss Alps, it felt like being transported into a western movie.

By the end of summer, I had passed the written, oral and flight tests with flying colours. I was a private pilot and proud to hold the certificate in my hands. Upon turning twenty-one a few days later, the family planned a party to celebrate my birthday and the accomplishment of the first step of what would become a long road to reach my aviation goal.

It was almost the end of my year, and another girl was due to arrive to replace me. After her arrival, I remained a little longer to help her settle into the routine. I gave her my room and slept on the floor behind the couch in the living room for a few weeks. I wanted to make this a smooth transition, especially for Jordana and Lacy as they had become attached to me during our year together. Finally, the day arrived and I said farewell to everyone and jumped in the plane dressed in my western outfit. I arrived in Geneva where my parents picked me up and walked out of the airport with my cowgirl hat on and my guitar in hand.

Unfortunately, it was back to reality, back to where everything was a year ago. The pain of Joel's death and the family dramas were waiting for me as if I had never left. I knew what I wanted to do with my life, but I needed support. I wanted to be a pilot, not just fly as a hobby; I couldn't afford that anyway. I contacted Chris, the other pilot who was on the trip when I had met Joel. I had maintained contact with him, and he had been at my twentieth birthday party, so he knew my parents as well. I discovered my mom had also stayed in contact with him and on occasion they had met for coffee while I was in California.

My mother drove me to the airport so I could meet Chris at the coffee shop. While asking his advice on what I should do next to achieve my goal of becoming a pilot, another pilot, Paul, joined us at the table. We talked for a while, and he invited me to join him on his next flight. The company was operating on single pilot crew meaning that if the plane wasn't full with passengers, there would be an empty right seat in the cockpit where I could sit and have a taste of what it is like to do this as a job. Of course, I was thrilled and jumped at the offer.

While driving back home, I asked my mom to stop at a store so I could buy an aviation magazine. Back in my room, I flipped through the pages containing aviation school advertisements and immediately applied to several for admission information. A few days later, I joined Paul on another flight where he let me take over the controls on the return flight that had no passengers. It felt so good. I hadn't flown since leaving California, and I was already missing it after only a few weeks.

Paul and I met on several other occasions, for flights and for a drink, and I realized he wanted to be more than just friends. However, I was far from ready to start another relationship. Joel was still in my heart, and I was planning to leave again for school anyway. Paul understood and accepted it—for now.

While waiting for a reply from various schools, I had to find financial assistance. To get my private pilot license I had to use the eight thousand Swiss Francs I had saved during my three-year apprenticeship. My year in California didn't have a salary, so I was broke. My parents were not against my plan, though I also knew I couldn't count on their help either. But thanks to Chris' advice and contacts, I was offered a scholarship. It was far from enough, however, so I secured a bank loan—a large one—to cover my schooling.

Upon receiving replies from schools, I decided to go with one in Arizona because there was a class for people like me who were requesting individualized training. They were also training future pilots for KLM, Lufthansa and Japan Air, so I knew it was probably a good school. I busied myself with the paperwork for enrolment, applied for a student visa at the US embassy, sent an initial payment for classes and booked myself a ticket to Tucson, AZ. Three months after returning from California, I was ready to head back across the ocean and work hard. It was difficult to say goodbye to my friends again, but I was relieved to escape the family drama once more. My brother was living his own life and pretty much cut out any contact with the family, so he had no idea what I was doing. And my parents could brag about their daughter becoming a pilot, so they did not oppose my career choice.

By March 1995, I was back in the US and on my own. All the students at the aviation school lived in apartments in the same complex. My class was very small as we were the only four who paid for their individual training to obtain the FAA Commercial Multi IFR Licences. But together with the classes of Lufthansa, KLM and Japan Air training, we filled a good part of the residency area. Male students shared two-bedroom apartments, and the few female students occupied small single-bedroom apartments. I had privacy, and for the first time in my life I felt like an adult finally living my own life. I was excited on this new adventure and very motivated to work for the next six months to obtain my commercial license. But most of all, I was happy and free, a feeling I hadn't felt since childhood. I was ready to take on the world again.

We had to complete the theoretical part of the course first, which took almost two months of daily classes. Once that was done and we had passed the written exams, we would finally start flying. In celebration, the other students and I drove to Phoenix for the weekend to attend an air show. It was the end of sitting in class and the beginning of the practical part we had been looking forward to for the past few weeks. The closest we had come to the airplanes we were going to fly was to watch other students on the tarmac from inside the school. But the frustration was coming to an end. It was our turn! Every weekday for the next four months we would team up with an instructor or another student to maximize flight time and complete solo trips as required.

But first we needed uniforms, which the school requested. Japan Air students had navy blue pants and white shirts. Lufthansa and

KLM students wore flight suits, either blue or grey. As individual pilots, we were required to purchase our own military green flight suits. For safety reasons, shorts and T-shirts weren't allowed as we were flying mostly in a desert environment. What better place than an air show filled with displays of all kinds and stores selling everything related to aviation and military surplus to find what we were looking for? We added the flag of our country of origin on one arm and the school provided the nametag. Now we were officially ready to fly the skies.

The school used Beechcraft Bonanza F33 planes. They were painted yellow and nicknamed "yellow bananas." They were so easy to recognize that most of the airfield personnel in the state of Arizona knew we were students when they saw them. It took a few flights to become comfortable flying it. Transitioning from the Cessna 172 I had flown for my private license, I now had a constant speed propeller plane with retractable gear to operate. But I loved this fast, low-wing aircraft; it was fun to fly.

Being based in Tucson at Ryan Airfield, we had interesting neighbours. Once in a while when doing manoeuvres in the training area, the military from Davis-Monthan Air Force Base would fly by above, beneath or play with us. After all, a little yellow banana makes a perfect target for an A-10 on a training mission, doesn't it? The A-10 is commonly referred to as the "Warthog" and was designed for close air support. Davis-Monthan was also a tourist attraction as a huge boneyard, a storage area for aircraft taken out of service. We enjoyed driving along the miles of fences and looking at the aircraft that had seen better days. We'd also visit Pima Air & Space Museum and talk aviation.

A typical day at school involved reporting in the morning for an hour-long briefing, preparing and taking the planes on our daily mission, and ending with a post-flight debriefing. We would alternate a day of instruction with a solo flight or a longer cross-country flight teamed with another student. When it was time to drive back to our living quarters, we contacted dispatch for the next day's schedule before returning to the apartment for a night of study. But first, we usually gathered around the swimming pool or played a friendly game of basketball to burn energy, or we chilled out by exchanging stories of what we had learned or experienced that day. Our weeks were full and intense, but we decompressed on weekends by getting together in one of the apartments or driving to town for a night out.

Paul wrote me on a regular basis. But I was too busy with my studying and having too much fun enjoying my freedom in Arizona to think about what was happening back home and his expectations. I wanted to forget it all and was contemplating staying in the US. Possibly sensing that I was slipping away, he decided to take a vacation right around the time I was graduating. He and his best friend were both pilots, so they planned to rent a small plane in California and fly from Los Angeles to Tucson. They wanted to pick me up and go on a two-week vacation flying across the west, visiting various national parks and making sure I'd return back home to my country.

I eventually passed my exams and graduated as a certified commercial pilot with instrument and multi-engine ratings, and my logbook contained three hundred hours of flight time. When Paul and his friend arrived, it didn't take long to put my luggage on-board their plane before we took off toward the north. I looked back one last time at the scene of what had been my home for the last six months and one of the best experiences of my life. After touring Arizona, Utah, Nevada and California for two weeks, and Paul vying for my attention, I flew back home with a sense of déjà vu.

CHAPTER 3

PILOT IS MY PROFESSION

Here I was, back home again. I had a professional pilot license, but it was useless to me because it wasn't valid in Switzerland or any other European country. Before I could even start looking for work in this field, I needed to convert my license. So it was back to school. However, I didn't have to do it all over again because it would have been pointless to have it done it in the US in the first place. I had to write a couple of exams, get simulator training and twin-engine small plane training to prepare for a check ride. In the end, it was still cheaper than if I had done it all in my home country. The trip to the USA, renting an apartment and a car and the six months of training in the flight school was still a bargain compared to the cost of this type of training in Europe.

During this transition time, I lived with my parents again. Not only was I broke, but I had a huge loan to pay back. However, I wasn't stressing much about it because I didn't have a deadline to repay. The only downside was that the interest would increase the longer I waited.

Paul was once again inviting me to join him flying when his trips were not full, and he even had it approved officially by his boss who gave me a proper uniform. The company also had a small Cessna 206 used mainly for sightseeing tours over the Alps. As luck would have it, they could fit in an additional pilot, so I had a foot in the door. It was also a good way to accumulate flying time. But all this came with no salary. I accepted and was given a pager that beeped when a flight was booked. I'd jump in my car and drive to the airport to prepare the plane, fill out the flight plan and meet the tourists. Off we would go for thirty minutes to one hour of flying over the beautiful Swiss Alps.

One day, I picked up a group of five people and led them onto the tarmac. After boarding the minibus and driving them to the end of the runway where the plane was waiting, I parked the bus and we disembarked. At that point, the passengers started to shake my hand and say thank you and goodbye.

"Ha, but I'm the pilot!" I said.

In a split-second, their smiles turned into confused looks. It wasn't the first time I had had "the look." But this time, I could actually see fear on some of their faces. With a big, bright smile, I did my best to find words to calm them down. I had to face this problem over and over again. As a twenty-two-year-old I was young, but I looked more like a fifteen-year-old. Of course people had to ask if I was old enough to fly. As frustrating as it was sometimes, it also made me laugh.

Flying over the mountains was magical, but it was also challenging for a relatively novice pilot. The weather can change very quickly; the wind often funnels into the valleys and it can get rough. But I quickly learned the patterns and best options for crossing ridges to avoid frightening my passengers with too much turbulence.

On a similar flight a few weeks later, I had four passengers on a bright, clear day that was perfect for sightseeing. It was Sunday and we levelled off at thirteen thousand feet, flying from Mont Blanc toward "Le Cervin" (the Matterhorn). I was concentrating on my flight path and constantly scanning outside for other small planes that often frequented the area on weekends. At the same time, I had to entertain my passengers and name the mountains, glaciers and lakes. Suddenly, I heard a "whoosh" and saw something flash in the corner of my eye. I looked around, behind, up, down, on the right, left. Nothing, it was already gone. Fortunately, none of the passengers noticed. They were all too busy admiring the view on the opposite side and talking to one another.

We continued on and eventually landed safely at the airport. I accompanied them to the terminal and they thanked me for a great flight. Only at that moment did it sink in. My knees started to shake as I realized how close I had come to a fatal accident. I reviewed what had happened over and over again, but I couldn't make sense of it. I had no idea where that plane had come from. I didn't see it coming at all. All I know is that it came pretty much from the opposite direction and that its wing tip came about a metre from my own. That was a close call and an experience from which I learned to be ever vigilant.

I was gaining flying experience for my logbook but was still far from the total flight time needed for most companies that were hiring. Paul was still flirting with me and never let up. Sometimes it was annoying, but it was also flattering and gave me an opportunity to breathe away from the suffocating environment at home. He was so persistent that I finally gave in.

"OK," I said. "Let's give it a try."

We started dating and saw each other more frequently. I was living with my parents and he with his mom. But I was still thinking of Joel. I missed him so much, though I knew I had to move on. Something disturbing happened one night after an evening at Paul's. Upon returning home, I looked in the mirror and noticed that even though I was still wearing the necklace Joel had given me, the small airplane pendent on it was missing. It had broken off from its hook. I panicked and started looking for it everywhere—inside the house, in the car, on the ground between the car and the house! Nothing, it was gone.

I looked relentlessly for days but never found it. Finally, one day while sitting on my bed, my eyes began to tear up. I couldn't stop crying. I remembered Joel saying, "You'll give it back to me the day we divorce." I hadn't taken the little airplane off for three years. I was devastated, but I saw it as a sign that he had taken it back. Time to let go.

In February 1996, I was excited about a two-week vacation to Florida—a must-visit before going home. Besides my passion for aviation, I had always been interested in space and the NASA program. During flight school, my favourite instructor in Arizona was just finishing a phone call one day when I walked into the office for my briefing. She said she was on the line with a very good friend who works at NASA Space Center in Houston. When I told her about my interest in space, and how impressed I was that one of the astronauts was Swiss, she gave me an address where I could write to him if I wanted. I did write. I didn't expect a reply, so I was shocked when I received a wonderful letter from him that included an invitation to visit Cape Canaveral for the launch of his next mission STS-75. I couldn't refuse!

The day before the launch, I visited the base and witnessed the space shuttle ready to move onto the launch pad. The orbiter itself is an incredible spacecraft, but seeing it attached to the massive size of the external tank and the two solid rocket boosters was impressive. The weather was perfect for launch. I had a seat at the closest location to watch the countdown. Everyone was excited as the clock finally wound down… 3, 2, 1 and lift off.

Gazing down a few kilometres across the swamp where the shuttle was located, I saw a white cloud surrounding it as it began to lift off. At first, it was quiet. But soon the noise travelled to us in the form of loud successive explosions. A chill ran up my spine and tears rolled down my cheeks. With a bright smile on my face, I could see that I wasn't the only one crying. It was an amazing experience and a day I shall never forget. My sincere thanks and appreciation go out to Mr. Nicollier.

Upon returning home, I moved into a rented chalet with Paul. I was freshly inspired and decided that no matter how difficult it was, I would never give up and would eventually fly for a living. I still had a long road ahead of me but believed my day would come.

I kept flying intermittently for the next year while housekeeping our home. In 1997, I took a two-month summer contract in a factory making watches on an assembly line to make extra money. Although boring and monotonous, it was nevertheless a job and salary I needed. At the end of the summer, it was back to school and my final step to acquire a written Airline Transport Pilot License (ATPL).

I needed an ATPL to land a good job in the airline industry, so I registered for this very intensive course. I drove for thirty minutes, took an hour-long train and a fifteen-minute subway ride to get to class. The course covered flight planning, air law, human performance, general navigation, instrumentation, weight and balance, meteorology and more. At the end of each day, I studied the whole way home on the train. Back home, I ate a quick supper, studied more and dropped into bed for a few hours of sleep. Rinse and repeat. No days off. By the end of the first month, I had completed half the subjects and wrote two days of exams. Then it was back to the same routine for a second month. It was the most intensive study I'd ever experienced, but I was determined to attain that license—I had to!

Soon after graduation, Paul had signed a two-year contract, and we planned to move to Madagascar. I was excited about a new adventure and a chance to discover the kind of life I had dreamed of ever since seeing *Out of Africa*. I was still a teenager when I saw it, and the life of Karen Blixen and Denys Finch Hatton, played on screen by Meryl Streep and Robert Redford, fascinated me. Somehow, I knew this was the kind of life I was cut out for, one to which I would constantly aspire in the future. Plus, I would be moving far away from my family where they couldn't control my life anymore. At least, that's what I thought....

First, I had to concentrate on exams, as I couldn't afford to fail a subject. Despite being allowed to rewrite some of them, I would be too far away to do so without inconvenience and expense.

Upon finishing the ATPL course, we prepared for our departure, packing, shipping our car and furniture ahead and completing the paperwork to become expatriates. I say "we," but I was mostly on my own when it came to organizing the packing and boxing all our belongings while Paul was at work.

When the letter with my test results arrived, I opened it nervously because I was convinced I had failed at least two of the subjects. My hands were shaking. As my eyes quickly moved across the printed page, a wave of relief washed over me as I read that I had passed all the exams. Amazing! I had done it.

A few weeks later, I was finally ready to start our journey to Africa after saying goodbye to friends and family. Paul's mom had already decided she would visit us after a few months, and his best friend took time off to join us on the trip and stayed for a couple of weeks to help us settle into our new life. This new adventure was a way to turn the page again, start fresh, and get myself out of that sadness I was feeling in my own country. Madagascar, here I come.

CHAPTER 4

THE BIG ISLAND

We left the wintry mountains of Switzerland and set foot in Antananarivo, Madagascar, on November 30, 1997. A quick flight south and we were in the town of Antsirabe, where we were based. What culture shock! The colours, smells and sounds—everything was different. What struck me most at first was the constant buzzing of life in the streets. There were people everywhere walking along the road. Little shops laid their wares out on the ground. The kids called out "vasa" (white people) every time they saw me. Everyone seemed friendly and always smiling.

Madagascar, the biggest island in the Indian Ocean, gained its independence from France in 1960. So many people, especially the elderly, still spoke French. This landmass separated from the mainland millions of years ago and evolved apart from the continent, so the majority of plants and animals are endemic to the island. Some can't be found anywhere else on Earth. Life there seemed much as it was on the continent based on what I had seen on TV documentaries about Africa. My first thought was, *I'm going to love it here!*

We lived in a company guesthouse while waiting for the container with our belongings to arrive. Paul started his job right away.

After two months of sitting around and waiting, I became frustrated and felt useless with nothing to do. The initial excitement at being there faded, and I was stressing out about how to start making money to pay back my loan and how to find a job flying again. Tension grew between Paul and me, and we had some intense verbal fights. This wasn't new, as we had already experienced some of this the year before. I was feeling trapped, and seeing him living his dream while I had to put mine on hold was making me sick, but I pushed aside my own desires to please him and did my best to swallow my anger.

Things finally started to improve when we moved into our own house. We met a private pilot who used his plane to transport people and who was looking for help. I immediately converted my licence to be able to fly and did a few short flights. It only required validating my private license, as I would not be flying for an airline but privately. This resulted in my first experience of corruption in Africa. I didn't have to take any tests, just a friendly talk with the person in charge of dispensing the license and slipping a bottle of rum under the table. That's Africa for you!

After completing a few flights for this person, Paul's boss heard I was also a pilot. The company, managed by a father and son originally from India, owned three aircraft. One of them was a Piper Comanche, a four-seat, single-engine aircraft mainly used for their own pleasure. The work-related trips were usually done with two twin-engine aircraft, a King Air and a Piper Chieftain. Eventually, I was made an offer I couldn't refuse. In an effort to help me out, the father decided that the Comanche would be used for smaller trips around the island when only one or two passengers were scheduled, and he offered me the opportunity to fly it. I wouldn't be paid for the service, but it was a way for me to build up hours in my logbook and stay current with my license. It felt good to be "employed" again, and I was finally able to put my training to good use and gain experience.

On my first flight, I stopped at the international airport to pick up a passenger whom I would fly to the cotton fields up north. We planned to fly in and out of three or four airfields where he supervised the progress of the farms. All I had were the co-ordinates of where the strips were located, but no charts or other information. They told me not to worry, as the superintendent coming with me knew the area very well. After an hour we finally arrived and, according to my GPS, I was right over the airfield. With a confused look I checked around but couldn't see an airstrip.

"Where's the airfield?" I asked.

"There," he said.

"Where?" I said.

"Right down there. See the road crossing the fields?" he replied.

"What? The dirt road with the tractor on it?" I said.

"Yes! That's it. That's where we land," he replied.

OK, I said to myself, spying a line of trees nearly fifty metres tall at the beginning of the road. When I pointed this out, he said, "That's OK, just fly over them and land."

That was going to be quite a challenge for a novice pilot like me, but heck, why not? I concentrated, prepared for landing and lined up with the road. All the while, I couldn't help wondering how much beating this retractable-gear, low-wing aircraft could take.

It couldn't be good for it to land on such airfields. I figured I had better not screw up this landing. Upon final approach, I ensured nobody was on the road and maintained enough altitude to clear the trees. I had to cut the power and dive right away to make it with enough space to stop. I flared, but not well enough, and landed hard onto the dirt. I slowed down and finally brought the plane to a full stop. I rolled my eyes with a forced smile, but my passenger said, "Well done!" I guess he was used to this.

I waited for the dust to settle before opening the door. Looking to my left and grabbing the door handle, I was startled by a man standing a few metres from the cockpit. He was holding a spear and had an animal skin wrapped around his waist.

"What the hell!" I yelled.

"Oh, don't worry about him," said my passenger. "The local people often come around to see us. Seeing an airplane is a wonder for them."

No kidding! I thought.

We flew from one cotton field to the next for the rest of the day. I spent the night at a farm, sharing my bed with insects and my toilet with amphibians. I was praying there were no snakes! I hate snakes! But man, I was happy, and I loved the whole experience.

Life was good again. I was settling into African life and truly enjoying it while getting to fly almost once a week. The only downside was that my health was suffering, and I was losing weight from being sick too often. Most times, I didn't even know what it was. After a few days of high fever, resting in bed and some home remedies, my health would rebound. There was no hospital, and the closest doctor we could trust was in Tana, the capital.

Antananarivo was a more than four-hour drive on a treacherous road, so it was not really an option. The plan was that if any of us got badly injured or sick, we would be flown to Reunion Island to a proper French hospital, but that was only in case of a major calamity.

Africa introduced me to many weird insects I had never seen before. We decided to cut down a tree next to our house because it was full of caterpillars, as our gardener said it was the only way to get rid of them. In doing so, the caterpillars released their clear, furry hair in the wind, some of which landed on my legs. The burning rash from my allergic reaction was not pretty. Both my legs turned bright red and the pain was unbearable. Alphonsine, our maid, told me to put water in the bathtub, add a bottle of vinegar and lay in it for as long as I could. I did, and what a relief! As long as I stayed in the water, the burning and itching stopped, but as soon as I got out, it resumed. This continued for nearly forty-eight hours of madness before finally abating.

Every couple of months the owner of the company we worked for would take his family to Reunion Island for a long weekend to relax, recharge, shop and stock up with food items not found in Madagascar. Paul usually piloted the plane, so I was invited to come along. It was a nice change and gave me the opportunity to visit the island. It's not big, so we could easily drive around it in one day. With the mountains, the volcanoes and the beaches, there was plenty to do over the weekend.

I also visited Mayotte and Mauritius, two other islands in the Indian Ocean. In Mauritius, all I got to see was the airport as we just dropped off passengers and returned home. In Mayotte, there was a beautiful blue lagoon with a beach where one could swim surrounded by big turtles. If we were lucky, we also saw lemurs, the only other place besides Madagascar where you can spot these amazing and beautiful animals.

One other destination on our list was Johannesburg, South Africa. We mainly went there with the King Air 200 on its maintenance schedule. When we were booked to do it, we usually stayed a week or so and took the opportunity to explore. We rented a car and drove to Kruger National Park. What a treat. It was my first experience of a game drive, a real safari! It was the winter season, so it was easier to spot wildlife without thick and bushy leaves on the trees. We spent three days and two nights in the park.

The drive started at six in the morning as soon as the gates that prevented wildlife from mixing with humans were opened. In the evening, the gates were closed again. We drove no more than twenty kilometres an hour, our eyes constantly scanning for movement. I saw elephants, zebras, lions and other animals in their own habitat. It was like the reverse of visiting a zoo—we were stuck in the cage (the car, that is). I fell in love with this continent then and there. The thought that Africa would always be part of my life rushed through my body with a burning sensation.

One day back in Antsirabe, I was scheduled to make a simple flight of about two hours in the Comanche to ferry a couple of people to a private lodge in Ranohira in the south of the island and return home. Madagascar is very diverse with forested mountains to the north, the remaining rainforest along the east coast, and swamps and mangroves in the west. It was my first time going south. The landscape changed from the high plateau of the centre where most of the vegetation had been replaced by rice fields, to a desertic land in the south where the famous baobabs can be found. The flight was smooth, but it was on my way back, alone and enjoying the view, that something caught my eye. It was like a dark cloud, but not in the sky. It was close to the ground, and it was moving! I had heard of a cloud of locusts before but never seen one. Every so often, an invasion would spread across the country, going from one field to the next destroying everything in its path. Despite being quite a distance from home base, and because they were moving north, I didn't worry about it and returned home.

A few days later, I was in Tana with the Comanche again while another pilot took the King Air. I decided to leave for home base in advance because his plane was larger, so it would take him no time to catch up. This way, we would land at pretty much the same time. When I started my approach to the landing strip, the sky turned dark again, and this time I realized what it was. The locusts had been on a constant move and had reached our region. They had already spread through town and were just about to cover the airfield. I radioed the King Air to let him know, and he said not to worry because he was right behind me. On final approach, the blue sky turned black. After landing and taxiing to the front of the hangar, I jumped out of the plane and ran toward the runway hoping to spot the King Air coming behind me.

The locusts had already covered the ground, stacking upon one another, creating a carpet of buzzing, crunching insects. Some were flying at my height and were swirling around my head. The King Air landed in the middle of this mess, but safely. The ground crew were in for a major clean up; the plane was covered with a yellow mashed mixture of what was left of those that had crossed its path.

The kids in town would run around trying to catch as many as they could. They really enjoyed the chase, and it was a free meal for them. They would fry and eat the healthy protein, thus filling their empty stomachs. They actually weren't bad at all. With seasoning, locusts make a good snack.

THE BIG ISLAND

A few weeks later, I was scheduled for a three-day trip to the east coast with several passengers. They were surveying the factories and offices at three different locations, and the trip continued from one location to another including overnights at each. One of those airstrips was very peculiar. A train track crossed the runway and, if a train came, it had to be given priority. Better make sure to look twice before landing!

At the end of a full day, I dropped my bag in a cute little bungalow that had been booked for me. The sound of waves crashing on the beach was like music to my ears, and I was looking forward to a peaceful night. Once refreshed after a cool shower, I headed to the restaurant for dinner. I was in a mood for a delicious seafood pasta plate, and what better place for one than right on the ocean? I enjoyed a chatty evening around the table with my passengers, had a wonderful meal and was happy with the perfect day it had been. When nightfall arrived, we said goodnight and retreated to our own bungalows. I tucked into bed and listened to the ocean while trying to fall asleep.

But something was wrong. I couldn't sleep and felt weird. Soon, my stomach started cramping. Feeling feverish, my head was pounding. I tried to get up, as I needed to find the toilet bowl quickly. My whole body started to shiver. I could barely stand on my feet. I crawled toward the bathroom and made it just in time. The pain finally let up after what seemed to be a long time sitting on the cold floor staring at the toilet. Returning to bed, I said to myself, *Breathe, breathe, you're going to be fine.* I just wanted some rest.

I looked awful the next morning and couldn't hide my exhaustion, but I told my passengers I was fine and that I would fly them to Toamasina where I was supposed to drop them off. After a very light breakfast, we flew along the coastline to enjoy the scenery.

It was the rainy season, and thunderstorms were building up fast by midday, so flying in the early morning was our best chance for a smooth flight. When I dropped them in Toamasina, I hoped to leave again as soon as possible to avoid the bad weather. Unfortunately, I was supposed to bring back cargo, and the truck was late. When it finally arrived, there were too many boxes and bags to fit on-board. We wasted more time figuring out which ones to load and which ones would remain behind for the next flight.

Meanwhile, a storm was building south of the airport, and it was moving in fast. My head was still spinning, and my body was weakened from the food poisoning the night before, but I dreaded staying another night. I needed to return home and take care of myself. I encouraged everyone to hurry so I could get airborne and finally took off with only minutes to spare. The thunderstorm moved in, but I managed to begin my on-route heading just in front of the dark wall that had begun flashing brightly with lightning.

I was on my way home. I still had a few hours to fly and found myself sandwiched between two layers of clouds. The stormy weather was above, but the low-level clouds completely obscuring the ground were what concerned me. If anything happened, I couldn't see where to attempt a landing. Eventually, my GPS said I was approaching Antsirabe, and should be over the runway in ten minutes. The clouds were still thick, and I had no visual sighting of the ground. Now what? I could divert to Tana—about thirty minutes—refuel there and wait for the weather to improve. I decided to keep going to see how it looked above the airstrip. As I flew across the little ridge east of town a few minutes later, the cloud layer finally dissipated enabling me to land safely. Home at last.

Paul was waiting in the front of the hanger when I rolled in. As soon as I stepped off the plane, he told me I would be refuelling and heading out right away for a flight booked at the last minute that morning. And it was another overnight. He saw the look on my face when I came closer, so I didn't have to explain that the state I was in made it impossible. He called another pilot to take over, and we drove home where I jumped in bed and slept for the next twelve hours.

Approaching the end of this first year, the coming year looked more promising. My boss offered to provide me with training on the bigger aircraft, the Piper Chieftain, that he used to fly around the island. I had done a few flights with it before and was excited about the idea of flying a twin-engine. It was just the experience I needed to build up valuable time in my logbook. Most companies require a certain amount of experience on multi-engine aircraft before being hired, so this was an amazing opportunity for me to get it without having to pay for flight time by myself. I was looking forward to another amazing year and wasn't thinking of ever returning to Switzerland; I had no attachment there. I was still calling my parents once a week, but they often made me feel guilty about something or other.

Just when I thought I would finally be able to get on with my life and enjoy the moment, Paul decided we wouldn't be staying a second year. He planned to break his contract at the end of the first one. I knew he didn't like living in Africa as much as I, but I never thought he would quit. His dream was to move to Canada. He had visited Quebec with his best friend a few times in the past and wanted to immigrate there. After some research, he secured the paperwork needed to begin the process to see if he/we would qualify. We filled out the forms and mailed them. While waiting for an answer, he started looking for work in Canada and contacted an agency that connected candidates with companies needing pilots.

CHAPTER 5

WHITE GIRL

Meanwhile, I was determined to complete all the flying experience I could in Madagascar. I knew that once we left, it could be months before I got another chance to sit in a cockpit. However, the Piper Comanche was due for a major overhaul and this couldn't be done on the island. The plan was to do a ferry flight to Johannesburg and have the facility maintaining the King Air do the work on it. Flying a small single-engine aircraft from Madagascar to South Africa is a little more complicated as I couldn't fly it straight across the ocean in one day due to its slow speed. Also, if I lost the only engine, well, you get the picture. I needed to take the long way around to make each leg over water as short as possible. I started planning my route considering the endurance of my fuel reserve, the weather and especially the wind. I also looked up what airport I was allowed to land to clear customs as I'd be passing through Mayotte and Mozambique on my way. The three-day journey was all a new learning experience for me.

On the first day, I flew to Antananarivo to clear customs at Ivato International Airport. That being done, I continued toward the northwest, flying over Mahajanga and then over water until I reached Mayotte. I had friends on the island whom I had met during previous trips, and they were waiting for me at the airport when I arrived. After spending a lovely evening with them over dinner, it was time to rest for the next day.

The second day, I started off with a long over-water crossing to reach the coast of the African continent. I had put on my life vest so it was ready for use in case of an emergency. Flying a single-engine aircraft over the water is stressful. I was constantly scanning the horizon for ships. If anything went wrong, I would do my best to crash-land as close as possible to one of them. I knew how big those container ships were, but they looked so small from high in the sky—like toothpicks floating in the ocean. I wondered where they were coming from and where were they going. What were they carrying in those containers? One of them had brought all our home furniture and our car a year ago. That made me remember I'd be shipping my belongings on one of them soon.

When I finally reached the coast of Mozambique, I removed the uncomfortable life vest from around my neck. The rest of the flight took me over sandy dunes, rivers, estuaries and lagoons before touching down in Nampula. It took a bit of negotiation to clear customs, as is often the case in many parts of Africa. Corruption is everywhere and any excuse is made to try to get money out of you.

After refuelling, I took off again and headed south toward Beira following the coastline for the most part. As it is the second-largest city in Mozambique, I was pretty confident it would be a good place to spend the night and find everything I needed. A bed and a warm meal.

Once the plane was parked and set for the night, I left the airport looking forward to a good night's rest. There was no hotel close by and no taxi to take me to the city centre, so I started walking toward a main road. I was approaching a group of men who were standing next to their truck on the road. One of them asked where I was going, and when I explained I was looking for a hotel, he offered to take me. Wearing a pilot's uniform often made people curious about me, but it also commands a lot of respect in Africa, and I felt a little safer than if I was just wearing plain clothes. With no other options and the sun beginning to set, I accepted his offer and sat in the front seat with the driver. I was not entirely comfortable with this situation, but it was still the better option than walking by myself in the dark. The rest of the group jumped in the back and everyone squeezed in. They were all curious and wanted to know where I was from and what I was doing. I wanted to know more about them as well and hear their stories, so we engaged in a friendly conversation. I was glad they helped me because it would have been a long walk to find a place to stay.

As we edged our way along the small streets of the town, I marvelled at the buildings that still carried the scars of the last civil war that ended in 1992. Suddenly, a rock landed on the windshield and shattered it. We jumped, and a sense of panic overtook our conversation. After we stopped, a few people started to walk toward the car and shout at us. When "my" guys shouted back, the mob came to a halt. I remained still, trying to make myself as small as possible, and waited to see what was going to happen. Luckily, the confrontation ended. When we finally drove off, they explained that someone had thrown the rock because they had a white person on-board. I was stunned and suddenly realized I was not always welcome everywhere. People in Madagascar were always friendly with me, but that was not the case here. Recent memories of war were still on everyone's mind. I just had to look around to see the scars. My "friends" dropped me off in front of a hotel, and I gave them money to repair their windshield. It was the least I could do.

Having settled into the room, I went downstairs to find a shop with food to bring on-board the next day. The manager of the hotel advised me not to walk alone, so he sent his guard to accompany me. I was glad he did, as I had to walk a few blocks to reach the closest store. Menacing pairs of eyes stared at us as we walked. People gathered around us, and I felt trapped as they closed in on me. I was probably overreacting, but I was a bit on edge after the windshield experience. While at the counter paying for food, a man approached me that the guard had to push away. Turning to see what was happening, the man was standing a few centimetres from me. When I saw him, I nearly freaked. He was disfigured and his mouth was not in a left to right normal position; it was at a right angle, his teeth aligned from nose to chin. It totally shocked me.

Back at the hotel, the guard offered to accompany me to dinner as well, but I didn't feel it was necessary. There was no restaurant at the hotel but, luckily, I only had to cross the street for a hot meal.

As night set in, I retreated to my room and was ready for a good night's sleep. It had been a long day. I fell asleep quickly but was awakened suddenly by loud shouting in the streets. I got up and looked out the window to see what was happening. A mass of people had gathered in the street, and it appeared some were fighting. Then everything blacked out; power had shut down and everything went dark. That didn't halt the fighting outside. I returned to bed to try and sleep again when the phone rang. It was well past midnight, and nobody knew I was there. Who would be calling my room? A voice on the other end of the line mumbled something about an "aircraft, yours, airport," and hung up. *What's going on?* I thought, becoming concerned. Worrying about the plane and trying to figure out what this was all about made it impossible to sleep that night. I wanted to leave this town as soon as possible.

I checked-out and returned to the airport at first daylight. Thank goodness the plane was where I left it. I paid for fuel and again negotiated the payment of taxes in the fixed-base operator (FBO) office. They wanted another immigration fee, but I explained I had already paid it in Nampula the day before. I even had the receipt to prove it. That didn't suit them, so they drummed up other fake fees to rob me of money: noise fee, traffic fee, parking fee.

"You've got to be kidding me?" I said.

Finally, we came to an agreement when I offered them the little money I had in my wallet and showed them the empty slot to prove it was all I had. I was glad I had hidden emergency cash in my shoes.

Back on the tarmac, I loaded my bags on the plane and did a meticulous pre-flight check to ensure nothing was missing. Everything seemed normal, so I climbed on-board and took off, relieved to be out of there and on my way to South Africa. After reaching cruising altitude about fifteen minutes later, I radioed my flight office in Madagascar to advise them of departure time and provide an estimate for destination. It was to be a four-and-a-half-hour flight, a good part of it over desolate land.

While talking on the radio, I heard a strange noise in my headset. I ended the call and performed a few checks to see what was happening, and it didn't take long to diagnose the problem. I had lost the alternator, which meant the battery was all that remained to run the electrical systems. Without the alternator to keep the battery charged, I only had two options. As I was flying in daytime and under good conditions, I could temporarily turn off all electrical devices. To save battery power, I could also turn the radio on only to call control at the designated checkpoints and use power only to lower the landing gear and flaps. However, I didn't know how good the battery was or if it would hold a charge during the remaining four hours. The other option was to return to Beira, call the owner and organize a rescue mission with a mechanic to fix the problem.

I thought it through and decided to keep going. As I'd never experienced a failure like that before, I was definitely nervous and stressed out, but I also knew that panicking would be of no help. Taking a deep breath, I forced myself to remain calm. I turned off all unnecessary electrical equipment and continued on my planned route. Before crossing into South African airspace, I turned the radio back on and checked the battery load, which seemed OK. I called control, declared a PAN-PAN—the international signal to declare an urgent situation but not yet a danger to anyone's life—and explained the problem I was encountering. After providing them an estimated time for my en-route checkpoints, I turned the radio off again. Control then just waited for my calls at the expected times. The flight went smoothly and, despite having to navigate through clouds, I arrived at the scheduled time at each point and finally approached Johannesburg four hours later.

I had to keep the radio on, as it was an area of heavy traffic. I notified the airport I was due to land at, and they prepared the fire trucks along the runway, just in case. The moment of truth came when I prepared for landing, lowering the flaps and landing gear. A lovely sound filled my ears when the motors started. Hearing the landing gear deploy and watching the flaps moving made me smile with a sense of relief. Pulling into the parking in front of the hangar, I shut down the engine and was happy to arrive safe and sound.

I explained what happened to the mechanic assigned to my plane, so he took a close look at the engine. When he inserted his hand in the engine cavity, pieces of the alternator crumbled in his hands. We looked at each other with surprise, wondering how that had happened. I couldn't help but think of the strange phone call I had received the night before. *Would someone really mess with my plane?*

A few days later, I boarded a commercial flight back to Madagascar, saying goodbye to my "little bird" as I knew I would never see or fly it again. The scheduled work to be done on it would take weeks, if not months, and I'd soon be leaving Madagascar for good, so it was a heartfelt goodbye.

When I got home, I busied myself with the big move, selling our appliances, furniture and the car. Again, I was packing as I had done a year ago in Switzerland, and I was pretty much on my own to do it again because Paul was at his office pretending to work; an excuse to avoid the drudgery of packing. Once our boxes were shipped to his mother's home, we said our goodbyes to friends and neighbours and headed to Tana for one last night.

Paul was too proud to admit to anyone in Switzerland that we were not returning to Madagascar for the second year of his contract. At least not right away. He wanted to stay with his mother for a couple of weeks and plan our move to Canada. He told his friends we were only in Switzerland on vacation and that we would be returning to Madagascar, which led them to believe that we had moved to Canada directly from there later on.

Although I wasn't comfortable with this lie, I played along to avoid trouble. His mom would take care of receiving our shipped boxes, and we would settle a few things before purchasing tickets to fly to Montreal. Meanwhile, he had already arranged converting his license to a Canadian one, believing he would get the job for which he had applied. I reminded him that it wouldn't be easy since all we had was a tourist visa and not a work permit yet. Landed immigrant status was still a far-away dream; we had yet to pass the first step to see if we qualified as new immigrants. But it didn't seem to concern him; he was sure it would all work out.

With my bags packed and airline ticket in hand, we headed for the Cointrin Airport in Geneva on a cold winter day. I had no idea what lay ahead. I just knew I regretted the prospect of not returning to Africa and, even more so, of not flying again for a while. A suitcase filled with clothes and a few personal items was all I carried with me, and it looked like this would be it for some time. As the plane took off, I closed my eyes and tried to hide the tears welling up.

CHAPTER 6

LOST BETWEEN THREE CONTINENTS

Montreal in the winter was a temperature shock. Finding ourselves in -20°C was quite a change from the tempered climate of Madagascar. I knew nothing about Canada, and the first thing I realized is that they were speaking a very strange French in Quebec. It made me smile and scratch my head as I sometimes struggled to understand the locals. We rented a car until we could find a more permanent solution and secured the cheapest motel we could find; money would be tight for a while. It was dark, cold and the neighbourhood wasn't what I had imagined. This set the tone for the lifestyle awaiting me for many months ahead.

We found a cheap apartment with a bed, a table, two chairs and a couple of plates and cups in the kitchenette. I didn't like it but tried to remain positive, telling myself things would soon improve. Paul attended the job interview but, as I had expected, he was turned away when they realized he didn't have a work visa. *Oh, what a surprise! I told you so!* I thought. Now what? Do we return to Switzerland? It was too late to return to Madagascar.

Paul stubbornly wanted to remain in Canada and get his Canadian license anyway. He thought we would eventually hear from Immigration concerning our application. The problem was we had only completed the first step, and there was no guarantee we would even qualify for immigration. That didn't matter to him, we were staying. Once he got his license, he started mailing out CVs, knocking on company doors and making himself known. But of course, the answer was always the same: "Come back when you have a work visa."

After two months in Montreal, he wanted to go west. We stopped along the way in every town to distribute resumes. I realized how big the province of Ontario was as it took two days to cross from east to west. Onto the prairies, fields stretched as far as my eyes could see. Wide-open spaces that had a certain kind of magic. Somehow we ended up in Edmonton, Alberta. God, that cold! I kept wondering if I was ever going to acclimatize to the winters in this country. I was used to snow growing up in Switzerland, but it was nowhere near as cold. Minus fifteen was considered a very cold day there, but the temperature dropped -20, -30, -40 in northern Alberta! How much lower could it get? We stayed there for two months and spent most days going to a job bank office for computer access and employment opportunities.

The rest of the time, we were becoming depressed in the small motel room we had rented on a monthly basis. Paul was spiralling, and I was doing my best to keep our spirits up. Some days, I had to get away and decompress, so I would walk in the frigid cold to West Edmonton Mall, the largest mall in North America. I spent hours just walking around, window shopping and dreaming about the things I couldn't afford. I sat and watched people ice skating on the indoor rink, or watched the dolphin show at the pirate's pool. It was a free show, so I could at least do that.

Paul finally accepted that we couldn't stay in Canada much longer and that we had to find work elsewhere. Remaining there would dig too deeply into our savings, so something had to be done.

A few weeks later, a company in Wisconsin, USA, offered him a job and invited him for an interview. He accepted, and we drove across several states with our few belongings. The day of the interview, we arrived early and drove to a nearby park while waiting. I was happy to be there because it felt like there might finally be light at the end of the tunnel. Putting aside my own aspirations, I thought at least Paul would be flying and able to work.

Suddenly, he totally lost it and broke into tears; he was a nervous wreck. I couldn't understand this reaction because he should have been happy about this opportunity. It had looked promising from the previous phone calls he had received. I gave him a pep talk, and he finally gathered his thoughts. I told him I would have given anything to be in his place and that he should be grateful just for the interview. He finally realized I was right and went in for the interview.

I was good at waiting in the car by then. Every time he had stopped along the way at places to submit his resume, I had to wait—sometimes hours—with the temperature dropping in the car. Tapping my feet and hands to keep warm, I would look out the window at people passing by, at aircraft manoeuvring on the tarmac and daydreaming. *Will I ever get a chance to fly again?*

He got the job, and we even had a place to stay right away because the company provided shared housing for their crew members and said we could stay there. The other pilots who lived there didn't seem pleased to have me around as I was not a direct employee, but once they discovered I was the perfect maid who cleaned up their messes every day, they grudgingly accepted me. My days were dull, and all I could dream about were the smells and sounds of Africa, the beautiful skies, the red earth and the adventures. I missed it so much. Spending most of my time alone drove me crazy, and it was very difficult to see Paul flying and having fun while I was bored out of my mind. However, I swallowed my pride and just pretended to share his happiness.

It was short-lived. Three months later, while doing the paperwork for his work visa, the aviation company said they were told the government had received their quota of visas for the year so they wouldn't be hiring for permanent positions at that time. As quickly as that, we loaded the car and hit the road. It was summer, and Paul missed the mountains, so we headed west to Colorado. To economize, instead of staying in motels, we scraped together our savings and bought a tent so we could camp in regional campgrounds while visiting tourist attractions along the way. Once in the Rockies, it was good to breathe the fresh mountain air and enjoy some hiking. The meadows were full of wildflowers and unimaginable beauty, but I couldn't lose sight of reality.

Before the end of summer, we were back on the road again in the opposite direction. Paul wanted to return to Wisconsin for the biggest air show in the world, Oshkosh. We spent a few fun days camping next to our car with thousands of other people and admiring the variety of aircraft on display or putting on a show in the air and on the ground. While it was relaxing, I was disappointed that Paul remained in denial. We couldn't keep on going like this much longer. We had been driving back and forth from Canada to the US every three months to get our passports stamped and maintain legal status as tourists, but it was time to wake up and face the reality: We needed work, and to get it we needed to leave North America.

Then some good luck fell out of the clear blue sky.

A company in Scandinavia, where a friend of ours worked, was in need of a crew to fly their Beechcraft 1900. The position was up for grabs, so we forged a plan to return to Europe. We first had to spend a few weeks in Wichita, Kansas, enrolled in a course on that type of aircraft. As luck would have it, the job offer wasn't only for Paul; I was offered one as a co-pilot! I couldn't believe what an amazing opportunity this was to finally jumpstart my career. I had only 660 hours of total flight-time experience, and the opportunity to fly a twin-engine turbo prop plane, with full employee status, was heaven sent.

After yet another long drive across the States, there we were sitting in a Kansas classroom and learning everything necessary to operate the Beech 1900. It wasn't easy, as this was my first time taking such a course. We covered detailed systems, electrical, hydraulic, engine, fuel and more, all within a couple of weeks. It made my head spin. The first week in class dealt with theory. The second week was spent in a level D simulator—a perfect replica of the actual cockpit—familiarizing ourselves with the aircraft and practicing emergency manoeuvres. The simulator sat on hydraulic jacks with full motion, flying exactly like the real plane despite being in a box on the ground.

I did my best but was totally stressed out. It was a lot to learn after being away from flying for a year. And it didn't help that I was assigned an instructor who seemingly couldn't stand me either because I was a young woman or because I was so inexperienced. Nevertheless, he gave me a hell of a time. But I successfully accomplished the training and arrived in Denmark, where the company was based, with my certificate in hand ready to begin my first paid job as a pilot. Our friend soon left this job and decided to return to his homeland, enabling us to take over his fully-furnished apartment and buy his car, so that worked out nicely.

After only a few flights, the company sent me with another captain to fly a King Air 200 aircraft based in England. At the beginning of 2000, I was flying newspapers between London and Dublin. I would fly all night and catch a few hours sleep during the day. My captain was originally from Australia, and he would sit on the steps of the plane playing the harmonica while waiting for the truck to deliver the newspapers. The plane wasn't set up to haul cargo. The company had removed the passenger seats enabling us to stack the papers nearly to the roof of the cabin. With no cargo net to secure them, we had to crawl over the stacks to reach the cockpit. I couldn't imagine the extent of the disaster in the event of a crash or a fire—it was crazy at best, possibly illegal at worst. It was a death trap. We flew in this manner for weeks. After complaining, we finally received cargo nets and were able to secure the newspapers and leave necessary space between them for proper exit access.

After a few months on the job, I was becoming comfortable with the routine when, out of the blue, Paul decided to accept a job with a different company. While I was in England, he had talked to other pilots about an interesting job based out of Sweden and, without discussing it with me first, had signed the contract. In no time, he had packed his bag and moved to Sweden, leaving me behind in Denmark.

It's times like these that I struggled to understand his thought process. He wanted me in his life, and yet he was acting as if I didn't count. Did he even realize what he was doing? Was I so naïve and oblivious to what a relationship was supposed to be that I accepted the way he was behaving?

When he finally realized his actions weren't fair, he gave me the address of their chief pilot so I could forward my resume. I was hired a few weeks later, but before I could start, I had to find someone to take over the rented apartment, sell the car and settle the bank accounts, among other things that adults have to do when they leave a country. When I finally arrived in Sweden, I made sure Paul understood that what he had done was not acceptable, and that he had better not pull another one like that.

We rotated two weeks off after a month of work and lived in a crew house. The whole organization was complicated. I was hired by a South African company to fly a Danish-registered aircraft that was contracted by a Dutch airline based out of Sweden, and I was flying scheduled runs to Germany. Pretty weird. My salary as co-pilot was small, $500 a month, but at least I was flying and building up valuable flying time on the Beech 1900D model. During our time off, we would give the house to the replacement crew and fly back to Switzerland to Paul mother's home. It wasn't the best solution, but it sufficed, and I enjoyed the work.

We settled into a routine once again, but less than six months later Paul decided to move on. He was offered a position to fly a jet in Switzerland.

"You've got to be kidding me!" I said.

"You can stay here and keep doing this," he replied.

"Oh, really?" I said.

If I hadn't known him better, I would have thought he was trying to get rid of me. Not so. He was selfish but, at the same time, wanted me with him—on his terms. I was so angry at having to put my career on hold again. His egocentric wants and needs were always final, and he had won again. I felt like I was back at square one. First, he left me for a month to live with his mother while he went to complete the orientation course for his new "toy." Then I moved into the tiny apartment he had rented in Bern, where he was based. I felt stuck in a fifteen-square-metre room for weeks on end, often alone, while he was away flying. I couldn't even speak the language there as I grew up in the French part of Switzerland and not the German one.

I was miserable and knew I had to do something about it. I couldn't continue living like this forever. It was time to find a job that I chose and not one dictated by following him all over the planet. I didn't want to stay in Switzerland. Just the thought of being there was making me sick. I wanted to return to Africa, so I concentrated my efforts on finding something there. I sent my resume to countless companies all over the continent—I was willing to go pretty much anywhere. Not many replied, and the ones who did mostly said "Thanks, but no thanks." Either I didn't have enough experience or they didn't need anyone at the time.

One day, however, I received a positive letter. A Moroccan company invited me for an interview saying they would cover most of the airfare to get me there. I accepted and, by end of 2000, packed a bag and flew to Casablanca, Morocco. I arrived on Christmas Eve to a room booked for me at a beautiful hotel. Another candidate joined me Christmas Day, and we enjoyed a tasty tagine, a traditional chicken dish, at the hotel restaurant. That evening back in my room, I contemplated all that had happened in the past year. Suddenly it dawned on me that this moment right now was finally something positive happening in my life. *It's about time*, I thought with a smile.

I went through the screening process, and the chief pilot asked if I would stay a few more days until the owner of the company returned from his holiday. That meant I would return to Switzerland after New Year's Eve, but heck, it's not like anything important was waiting for me there anyway. I accepted and stayed. A few days later, I finally met with the boss, and he offered me a position. I accepted without a second thought. All I had to do was return to Switzerland and pack my things.

Paul approved of my choice and agreed it could be a great experience, so I flew back to Casablanca two weeks later. The company covered the cost of a hotel room for the first two weeks, so I had to find a place of my own quickly. I searched ads and talked to people, and I soon found a small apartment in the Ain Diab area, close to the beach. It was nice to be able to walk on the beach and relax at the end of the work day.

First came the paperwork and, as usual, study and exams to convert my license. The first step was to request a student permit, which required taking the train to the civil aviation offices in Rabat a few times. Once I was ready to fly, I returned to the company's office at the airport, dropped off a copy of my permit and asked when I might be scheduled to fly. The answer wasn't very clear. I was basically told to come back in a couple of days. I went back every other morning for the next few weeks. Other expatriate pilots advised me to be patient and said work would eventually arrive. They said it was a slow process, and some waited nearly a year.

A year?

I thought they were joking, but they weren't. I have patience, but I would only receive 50% pay until I officially started work, which wasn't enough to cover the cost of my apartment, utilities, taxi and train rides. Plus, I had to eat! However, I needed this job, so I hung in there hoping to somehow manage. I'd been through worse, so it wasn't a big deal. I was eventually told they were awaiting the arrival of other candidates and that training classes would start as soon as they arrived. OK, that sounded fine with me.

I learned that aside from the turbo-prop aircraft I was supposed to fly, the company was looking into acquiring a couple of jets as well and were in the process of searching for qualified crew members. I told them about Paul and notified him about the prospect. Because I had followed him every other time, I thought it might now be his turn to join me. He sent his resume and was invited for an interview, which he accepted. After the interview, he stayed with me for a few days. They had apparently made him a good offer and, while he packed his bags to return to Switzerland, he told me he declined it. I later learned he never intended to leave his present job. The interview was just an opportunity to spend a few days in Casablanca.

OK then, so be it. But I was staying. I wanted this job and wanted to fly. I wasn't about to return with him to sit in the tiny studio while he flew every day. That's what I was thinking, but I never said it out loud. He left, and I went back to my waiting game.

After several more idle weeks, nothing materialized, and I began to believe that I might have to wait for a year before reaching the cockpit too. It was frustrating, and I was losing hope. Why was I having so much difficulty starting my career and finding a stable position? Was it ever going to improve?

It will! I kept telling myself. I just knew that some day things would turn around. I was prepared to wait.

After utter boredom for a couple of months, Paul called to say the immigration papers for Canada had arrived! We had begun the selection process over the past couple of years and had an interview with the Délégation du Quebec. He didn't have enough points to qualify, but I did. Because we were considered a couple (even though we were not married), they accepted him too. There were more questionnaires to fill in, this time from the Government of Canada after the approval of the Quebec services, and several more papers to acquire. After months of patience and bureaucracy, it was official.

I realized I was wasting my time in Casablanca and, for the benefit of our relationship, I decided to return to Switzerland and prepare a move to Canada. I tried to convince myself that I could start a new lifestyle with Paul that would last this time. We would live there, and I could convert my license and find a job flying out of Canada once we were settled. I left Morocco feeling disappointed about this failure because I had wanted to prove that I could do it on my own. *Next time maybe!* I thought.

CHAPTER 7

WELCOME TO CANADA!

Paul had already resigned his position in Switzerland, and we lived with his mother again for the few weeks until we organized the move. I realized something had changed and, even though we were celebrating this prospective new adventure, something was different between us. He was getting upset at me for no reason and in ways I had never experienced before. I felt he was pushing me away, which didn't make sense. Why would he immigrate to Canada with me? He had been spending a lot of time with Isobel, the former wife of his good friend Mark, who had recently died. But I thought it was to give her and her three-month-old baby some extra support.

Apparently, Paul was in the habit of spending time at her place over the previous few weeks, and when I returned, I began to accompany him. I was uncomfortable because of my tense relationship with Paul, but also because I found him a bit too comfortable with Isobel and the baby. It was almost like they had become family. It hurt because there was a time when I was feeling ready to have a family of my own, but he never wanted to have kids and made it clear to me, so I had dropped the idea of ever becoming a mother. The scene unfolding before me with Paul and Isobel was devastating. Once again, I swallowed my feelings and pretended all was fine; we were to leave soon enough anyway. But not before one more clash.

We started fighting about stupid things. Once while driving, he suddenly pulled over on the shoulder. He looked at me and said, "Sometimes I feel like I have to drag you everywhere and that you're attached to my leg like a ball and chain!" I was speechless and couldn't believe what I had just heard. After everything I had done for him—after the struggles and sacrifices so we could be together like he had wanted—hearing this hit me like a ton of bricks. I didn't know how to react or what to say. *I should open the door and walk away forever*, I thought. But where would I go—and how? I had nothing! I had nobody to count on for support. It was too late to return to Morocco, and the move to Canada had already been organized and paid for. I decided not to react and remained quiet. We didn't speak for the rest of the day, but I knew by the next morning we would move on by simply ignoring what had happened. Great way to build up resentment, isn't it?

With this crisis behind us, we said goodbye to friends and his mother and hopped a train to the airport. Spring had arrived in Montreal in May of 2001, and the weather was nice. I felt much better than on my first visit to this country. At immigration, we stepped into a special office for newcomers, and it took only a few minutes before we were released with a "Welcome to Canada!" That was it; I was now a landed immigrant. This was my new home and an opportunity for a fresh start.

Our friend who had helped us find the job in Denmark lived just outside Montreal. He and his wife invited us to stay with them as long as we needed. It was great. We had a beautiful place to stay while processing the paperwork for driver's licenses, medical services, bank accounts and credit cards, etc. It amazed me how fast and efficient the bureaucracy worked in this country. I had already experienced enough elsewhere to declare, "Canada is great!" We were both happy, and our relationship took a turn for the better again.

After a few months without a job offer, we hit the road again and crossed the country in five days. Once again, Paul dropped off his resume everywhere he could along the way. We spent the summer in Vancouver and stayed with a friend of a friend to save money. We didn't want to rent an apartment until we decided where to settle down, and that depended upon the work we could find. I started looking for a job, too, but not in aviation, not until my license was converted. I gave him priority again and waited until he found a job in aviation and we were settled before applying for my license.

By mid-August, he finally had a firm offer to fly a King Air starting in mid-September. It wasn't in Vancouver, though, but in the northern Alberta town of Peace River. Checking the map revealed that it was located about a four-hour drive from Edmonton, where we had stayed a couple of years ago.

We still had a few weeks in Vancouver before his job began, and my brother was planning to visit us soon. I hadn't seen him for quite some time, so it was good to reconnect. On a bright, sunny day, we arose early because we planned to visit the aquarium in Vancouver. When I walked into the living room, my brother was making breakfast and Paul was looking at a picture on the computer.

"Wow, look at this!" he said. "Whoever faked that picture did a pretty good job!"

He had a shocking image on his computer. Meanwhile, my brother had turned on the TV and immediately saw the same picture on the screen. It wasn't fake! It was real, and it was happening right now! September 11, 2001.

There's no need to explain what happened that day. Everyone on this planet with access to media clearly remembers where they were and what they were doing when it occurred. Walking the streets and gazing at the sky that day was very memorable. The Vancouver sky usually buzzed with aircraft flying in and out of the international airport and small floatplanes shuttling between the mainland and Vancouver Island. Not so today; it was dead silent. The sky was blue, no misty clouds trailing flight paths today. Air traffic was grounded all across the continent.

Still trying to process this tragic event the next morning, I said goodbye to my brother as Paul and I were leaving for Peace River. I enjoyed the drive and wondered if we would like our new town. Coincidently, we had a friend who lived in Peace River. With his help, I already had a job lined up and was due to report to the Travellers Motor Hotel for a position as front desk clerk. OK, it wasn't my dream job, but it was work. I was happy about it and didn't think twice.

We soon realized that things were changing drastically in aviation after 9/11. Paul had been lucky to secure a position just prior because from then on, many pilots found themselves unemployed as airlines were shaken up. The whole aviation world was affected by this tragedy, and it took a few years to bounce back.

Because of this, I had put a hold on converting my license for the time being. I believed I would fly again soon and would never give up on this profession, but it had to wait. Flying was what I was born to do, where I was supposed to be, so I was certain I would eventually get back in the air no matter how many more detours were ahead. I also knew I would return to Africa, as I had left a piece of my heart there.

But for now, I was in Peace River, a town of about six thousand that sits on the banks of a river called—you guessed it—Peace River. The landscape is fairly flat with small rolling hills, and the communities surrounding it are diverse with First Nations, French-Canadian farmers and Mennonites. It was already the beginning of winter and getting cold—very cold—and dark. The days were short. We settled in a two-bedroom apartment about a twenty-minute walk from the hotel where I worked. Paul was on-call most of the time, as his job involved ambulance flights. Because he never knew when a call might occur and only had one hour to reach the airport when an emergency arose, he had to keep the car handy. Once in a while, he dropped me off or picked me up from work, but I usually walked, even in -40°C weather. I bundled up in winter clothing with my hotel uniform underneath.

The work wasn't difficult, and I learned quickly on the job. Sometimes dealing with the customers was difficult. In addition to a restaurant, this 149-room hotel also had a lounge, a bar and a liquor store. A lot of rowdies came and went. I preferred the morning shifts from 7 until 3 in the afternoon because I was mostly processing checkouts, and it was more peaceful. The evening shifts, from 3 to 11 at night, involved mainly check-ins.

I was soon asked to do the night shift from 11:00 pm. to 7:00 a.m. By then, most of the hotel guests had checked-in and only a few early checkouts had to be done on this shift. But the bar closed at two in the morning, and not many nights passed without having at least one troublemaker. The only other staff person in the complex at night was the janitor. Around the time the bar was due to close, he remained in the lobby with me so I wasn't alone if drunks arrived. A security company patrolled the town each night, and the officer would check the hotel and stop at my desk several times. It was a good time for a coffee break with him and the janitor.

But by the end of the winter, I could leave the apartment with just my uniform and jacket because the weather finally improved. Despite being -10°C, it nevertheless felt like spring. Kids were playing outside in shorts and T-shirts.

One night on that job was particularly rough. It started with a customer trying to bring four young First Nations girls to his room. Realizing what he was up to, I tried to intervene. I politely explained that no visitors were allowed after hours. Of course, that wasn't going to stop him. So my friendly smile disappeared, and I became firm. He was most likely under the influence of drugs and alcohol, and he became aggressive and lunged at me. The bar manager nearby noticed the commotion and jumped between us to protect me. A few seconds more and the drunk would have decked me. That was the part of this job I hated the most. One positive thing I derived from this incident and so many others was that I learned to stand up for myself and say "No" to people. The shy and introverted girl I used to be changed that year. I became stronger mentally and emotionally.

At the end of that rough night, I left the hotel and walked into the parking lot. The cold hit me hard. It was a drastic change from the mild weather the previous day. I looked around to see if, by chance, Paul had come to pick me up. But I didn't see the car and started walking. It was beautiful out. The sky was pitch black but with the beautiful aurora borealis dancing above my head. What a spectacular sight. I started to panic about halfway home because I couldn't feel my legs. My face hurt, and I couldn't bear the freezing temperatures. I looked around hoping for a car to wave down, but with no one in sight, I kept moving while I cried with pain. All I wanted to do was get home and go to sleep.

When I finally arrived home, I saw the car parked in front. I was surprised to see that Paul was home as I thought he had been scheduled for a flight. When I opened the door, it was dead quiet. He was still in bed. I was fuming. *Why didn't he come to pick me up?* When I undressed, my legs were purple, and I couldn't feel them. I put my pyjamas on and went into the bedroom. As I walked in, he awoke and said, "Good morning. I didn't feel like getting up." I was so angry that I just ignored him and went to sleep.

Summer came and went as quickly as it had arrived. The nice thing about it was that the days lasted seventeen hours; I could still see some daylight at midnight, and it was sometimes difficult to sleep because my internal clock had been disrupted. I had been working at the hotel for a year, and the constant change of shifts from morning to evening then to nights caused further disruption to my body. It was disorienting, and I found it hard to readjust, so I made my boss a proposition. Nobody liked the night audit (overnight) shift, so in order to get my body into a solid circadian rhythm, I volunteered to do it full-time. Despite having trouble sleeping during the day, I at least would be on a stable schedule with no need to readjust.

I worked nights and slept several hours during the day throughout my second winter. With only a few hours of daylight, I mostly lived in the dark and didn't see much of the sun or blue sky. When I saw my picture for "Employee of the Month" a few months later, I realized how sickly I looked. I was as white as a zombie and had dark circles under my eyes. I was exhausted and started to hate the job. On the upside, I had finally managed to pay off my debt, with interest, after years of struggle. To celebrate, I used my first salary after the debt was repaid to purchase the best mattress I could find. One of Paul's colleagues had given us an old futon when we first arrived in town over a year previous, and we had been sleeping on it on the floor ever since. I had been struggling with back pain for months, but Paul found it fine so it meant there was no need to spend money on a bed.

One weekend, our friends from Quebec visited. They had only stopped for two days while doing a tour of the west, so Paul wanted to spend time with them and show them around. He had the week off, so it was good timing. I was still working the night shift.

"That's OK," he said. "We'll pick you up at 7:00 in the morning. After your shift, you can change at home and we'll have breakfast and visit."

"OK, but when am I going to sleep?" I said.

"You can sleep in the car while I drive from one location to the next," he said.

How insensitive! But I went along with it as I was also very happy to finally get to visit the region, play the tourist and have some fun. All I'd done so far was work and sit at home. Needless to say, after forty-eight hours with them, I crashed and didn't wake up till my body was refreshed.

A few months later, Paul was being his usual self and causing trouble at work again. I knew what was coming, and sure enough he lost another job. I was just biding my time and looking for any chance to get out of Peace River, so I mailed out resumes to hotels in more hospitable places like tourist towns in the mountains that were generally free of drugs, alcohol and rednecks. A response from a hotel in Canmore, Alberta, a town located just outside Banff National Park and an hour drive from Calgary, came back positive, so I accepted the job. *Perfect*, I thought, *I'll get to see the mountains again*. I moved back south, and Paul followed me, of course, as he was now unemployed. With this move, I bore the sole financial responsibility.

CHAPTER 8

THE BEAUTIFUL ROCKIES

loved Canmore. The view of the mountains surrounding the town was breathtaking. Working at the Rocky Mountain Ski Lodge felt like a vacation compared to Peace River. The owner was also Swiss, though he had immigrated long ago. I guess that influenced my getting the position. The front desk manager was a wonderful lady who was a few years older than me. She lived by herself and enjoyed the outdoors with her dog. I admired her freedom, and we became more friends than co-workers. I was enjoying life again, despite having put my goal of flying on hold. I knew that would eventually materialize, and I wasn't giving up on my dream even if I was not able to keep my licenses current for now.

I began working days, so I lost my "vampire" white face and felt alive again. On days off, I hiked in the mountains or took a thirty-minute drive to Banff, a resort town surrounded by the imposing peaks of Mt. Rundle and Mt. Cascade inside the national park. The town is nestled in 6,500 square kilometres of parkland and home to numerous wild animals including grizzly bears. Millions of visitors come from all over the world to visit. In the winter, the trails were also open for snowshoeing, something fun I had never tried before.

I began to realize it was difficult to get away and share time with someone outside my relationship with Paul. I had never had real friends or built a social life because we were always moving around. Besides a few times during the first year of our relationship, Paul and I never went out to restaurants, movies or anything that would allow me to meet other people. I became more frustrated with our relationship around this time. Paul had been sitting at home collecting unemployment for almost a year, but that soon ran out. He was looking for work as a pilot, but nothing was forthcoming. Every time I brought up the possibility of finding something in another field, his answer was, "No, I'm a pilot and I'll find a job as such." I was upset at his stubbornness. I was a pilot, too, but I found other work because we had to pay the bills. Why couldn't he? As usual, I didn't say anything and told myself to let it go; I didn't want to fight anymore.

Then came the discussion about buying a home. While exploring towns in the Rockies, he got the idea of settling in Golden, British Columbia, which was on the other side of the mountains. It was evident we could never qualify for a mortgage based on my salary alone, but, as always, when he made up his mind, it had to be done. He contacted a real estate agent in Golden, and we went house hunting on numerous occasions. Eventually, he fell in love with a huge house located thirteen kilometres outside of town. It was nice, an idyllic spot for a hermit. There were no neighbours as the property was a forty-three-acre forest. I tried to tell him that we should probably look for something smaller and closer to town, but it was like talking to a wall; he had already decided this was the one.

When it was obvious we couldn't afford it, he continued looking for work as pilot, but now he was looking for positions outside Canada. *Oh boy, here we go again*, I thought. Sure enough, he was hired for a posting overseas with Air Serv International, a non-profit humanitarian organization that flies relief workers and supplies to the most remote and challenging areas in the world, and the company I had always wanted to work for. *You've got to be joking! No way*, I thought. That job was supposed to be mine. Ever since I started flight school, I dreamed of flying for Air Serv in Africa and the Middle East. Being able to combine my love of flying with helping people who needed it the most was what I had always wanted to do. And he got it, even though he hated the idea of working under the harsh conditions of this job. I was so jealous. The position wasn't for Africa, though, as he probably wouldn't have accepted it had it been there.

The war in Iraq opened a lot of work for humanitarian and security workers. Paul signed a one-year contract for a posting based in Amman, Jordan, and flying to Iraq on a daily basis at the beginning of 2004. With the position secured, he signed the first offer to purchase the house once confirmation from the bank was received that a mortgage was approved. We moved out of our apartment in Canmore, and I moved into staff accommodation at the hotel. The owner of the lodge agreed to let me store our furniture in the basement of his house, right next to my staff room, until I could move it to our new home in Golden.

And just like that, Paul left.

I have to admit, I was almost relieved for this break. I thought the time apart would be good and our relationship would solidify once we got back together. I kept busy at work but was also overloaded with the process of purchasing the house. I had never done this before, and he left me alone to handle it all. Also, Golden was not just a move next door. It was a two-hour drive across a notoriously dangerous pass to the other side of the mountains. I found myself driving back and forth numerous times to meet with the real estate agent, insurance agent, lawyer, bank, etc. I had to prepare the paperwork and FedEx it to the other side of the world so Paul could sign and ship it back to me. It was a stressful process.

When the paperwork was completed, it was time to organize the move. I had already spent a few weekends cleaning the house, and now I had to rent a truck and load everything on my own to move in. I called U-Haul in Calgary and booked a fourteen-foot truck for the following weekend. The night before, they called me to say they didn't have a small truck but a seventeen-foot one was available. Having little choice, I agreed. I had never driven a truck that big before but thought I could figure it out. It couldn't be that difficult, could it?

The next morning, a friend dropped me off at U-Haul. As I walked into their office, the clerk said he was sorry, but the truck had broken down the night before. The only vehicle left was a twenty-eight foot one. I thought *Oh God, why does this have to happen to me?* Seeing my disappointment, the clerk told me not to worry. It was just a little longer but drove the same way as the smaller ones. Well, I had to get on with the move, so what the heck! He gave me the keys, I signed the papers, thanked him and went to find my chariot. I climbed into the cabin, made some adjustments and started the engine right away to avoid letting fear take over. I rolled onto the street as smooth as silk and drove off. As I approached the first intersection, it suddenly dawned on me that I was in the middle of the city and had to navigate in heavy traffic with busy intersections. *Ok, think.* I had a few metres of vehicle behind me, so I had to widen my turns. And when I did,

I surprisingly found myself driving this big truck with ease and enjoying it. This was fun! I felt big, strong and powerful.

I arrived in Canmore and started loading the truck with boxes. When it came to loading the big furniture, I couldn't do it on my own, so the other staff at the hotel came out to help. I was so thankful for this great team with whom I worked and lived. After a good night's sleep, I was ready to get back on the road and make my way across Banff National Park, through the pass, and finally unload everything in my new home. The assistant manager used his day off to follow me in his car and offered to help me unload the truck. After that, I needed to drop off the truck at the local U-Haul and drive back to Canmore with my boss for my shift.

At one point during my drive, I had to slow down because there were a few cars stopped along the way. I soon realized they were tourists watching a bear walking along the road. Since I had seen bears many times before, I wasn't going to stop and waste time. I drove slowly around the cars and kept going. As soon as I passed the line-up of tourists, the bear decided to cross the road and continue on his journey, so I had to stop as he walked right in front of my truck. I admired this beautiful animal from several metres away while everyone behind me had to look at the back of my truck. It was a precious sight for me, but not so much for those behind.

Because I was now living in Golden, my days at the hotel were numbered. What would I do? It had been four years since I had touched an airplane, and I hadn't even managed to convert my license because I hadn't had enough money. I didn't have my own bank account in Canada because Paul had insisted on a joint one that pretty much became inaccessible to me. He insisted on managing the finances himself, and he monitored the account closely. I even had to hand him receipts for a loaf of bread. He became obsessed with money. He was also convinced that he would win the lottery to renovate the house—and there was a lot to be done as the house was not finished and required much upgrading. But being short of cash didn't stop him from buying a big fancy truck. How was I going to save enough to convert my licence working a job that paid $12 an hour? The only option that returned me to flying was to look for work elsewhere.

"What if I sent my resume to your chief pilot?" I asked Paul one day. "Would they consider me despite not having flown for four years?"

Surprisingly, he agreed with my request and spoke to his manager in Amman. I forwarded my CV and a second copy to their office in the US and received the surprising news that they wanted to interview me. This was an opportunity I couldn't miss. I prepared myself as much as I could and flew to Virginia for the interview that was scheduled over two days. I met different people and was briefed on what they do and what they look for. I was honest about my background and the fact that I didn't have recent experience. I also wanted to ensure they considered me as an individual and not as Paul's partner. This lack of affiliation was important given Paul's tendency to create problems at work that often lead to him quitting or being fired after a few months. With the interview over, I headed back to Golden with the understanding that I would hear from them within a few weeks.

I returned to my work at the hotel and my basement apartment in Canmore. My manager, and now good friend, knew about the interview and, even though she hated to see me go, she was hoping it would work out given how much it meant to me. The very next day, Air Serv offered me a position. Furthermore, I was told they hired me because I had impressed them and not because of my relationship with Paul. They also said they had a policy of not sending members of the same family on the same project, but because they needed me for the Jordan-Iraq program, I would be flying the same route as Paul was. However, I would be scheduled to fly with other captains, consistent with their policy of not having members of the same family on the same aircraft. That was just fine by me. Live together but work with others was the way it should be anyway. It kept work and our relationship separate as much as possible.

I resigned from the hotel and started to organize things before leaving. The house was to be left empty and, with no caretaker, I had to ensure it was well secured.

I was very excited! After what seemed like endless patience on my part, I was going to work at my dream job.

CHAPTER 9

SPIRAL OVER BAGHDAD

Air Serv sent me to Colorado for simulator training to brush up on my skills and update my FAA license. Then it was on to South Africa to obtain license validation since the aircraft I'd be flying were registered there. I was given books to study for the written tests and introduced to Dale, the person who would complete my flight check. He ensured that I understood he was going to be stringent during the oral exam and the in-flight test, which set the tone for the next few weeks. Later on, I learned this rigorous introduction was designed to protect their pilots, as they wanted to keep using their own instead of having Air Serv pilots flying their planes. It was very political. I understood this, but there was no need to make my life miserable in the process. I just wanted the same as any other pilot: to make a living in this line of work. Years ago, Joel had described his work environment as a "basket of crabs," and I grasped the full extent of this meaning as my career progressed; competition always runs fierce in aviation.

I religiously studied the two huge binders of information I was given and registered for the tests when I was ready. I also participated in a week-long seminar for crew resource management, dangerous goods and a couple of other certificates. Once this was completed, it was time for the flight check. Since I didn't have a chance to do any flight training preparation beforehand, I had to count on my brief simulator training in Colorado. Although the simulator was not set up as a Beech 1900 but as a King Air, it was close enough since it was more about reviewing scanning and instrument flight rules (IFR) procedures. I knew this was not enough to really feel comfortable and that it would take a few days of flying to feel at ease again in the cockpit, but I didn't have that luxury. I needed to pass this test and knew it was going to be a rough ride with this check-airman.

They didn't have their own plane on site, so they managed to secure one from another company doing cargo flights between South Africa and Botswana. The only time the plane would be available was in the middle of the night. I was picked up at the hotel around 10:00 p.m. and driven an hour south to Johannesburg International Airport. After an hour of briefing and quizzing on all the plane's systems and sweating it out during the oral part of the test, we walked onto the tarmac and boarded the plane. I prepared myself in the cockpit with Dale in the left seat. He didn't forget to remind me, once more, that I was fortunate to be there given that I hadn't flown for the past four years. After starting the engine and doing the necessary checks, he handed me the controls. I taxied to the end of the runway for departure and took off well past midnight. The flight was to take an hour and a half.

Strangely, as we flew, his attitude changed. He presented me various failure tests to address, and we did a few different approaches to a nearby airport before coming back for a final landing at our initial point. Without a word, we disembarked and walked back to the office for debriefing. He was so quiet that I wondered if I had failed. But as soon as we sat down, he shook my hand and said, "Well done, you passed." He added that he was impressed by how well I had done given my long absence from the cockpit. I wanted to jump with joy, I was so happy, but I just smiled back and said, "Thank you."

I just had to wait for the civil aviation authorities to issue my validation. As soon as I received my papers, I was back in a plane, this time heading north toward Jordan. Paul was waiting for me when I walked out of the airport, and we were happy to be together after a few months apart. I was looking forward to spending time with him again, even if it was only evenings after work. I dropped off my luggage at our accommodation and went to the office. That's when he delivered the news.

"I'll be able to stay with you for the next two weeks so we can catch up, but then I'll be going back home to Canada," he said.

"You're kidding. Is this a joke?" I said.

Nope, it was true. He had messed around and they decided to let him go, so he was no longer working for Air Serv and couldn't stay there with me. He had done it again. Unbelievable! He was supposed to leave the very next day, but the country manager allowed him to stay in the apartment with me for a couple of weeks, as he knew we hadn't seen each other for a while. What was I supposed to do? I wasn't turning back and following him home. Not this time. This was a huge opportunity for me, and I was determined to make the most of it.

As I didn't have to start right away, we visited Petra and the Dead Sea. Petra is an amazing archaeological site where the structure of the city is cut from the rock. It's believed to have been established in the early 300s BC but remained unknown until discovered in 1812 by a Swiss explorer. The Dead Sea is 429 metres below sea level, and the salinity is about ten times greater than the ocean, which makes swimming impossible; you just float. The slightest cut would burn from the salt. With the water only up to my ankles, I flipped on my back and 90% of my body was out of the water. I laughed while I floated there reading the newspaper.

Two weeks later, Paul and I said goodbye and I settled into my new life. The company had three Beech 1900Ds, all of which were flying every day, all day. A typical day involved being picked up early to join the rest of the crew. They were contracted by the South African company and had separate accommodations. We drove to Marka Airport, the civil aviation airport three kilometres from city centre. While waiting for the passengers to arrive, I did the paperwork while the captain readied the plane for take-off. Aside from a flight plan, weather report and security report, we needed a unique, daily transponder code to enter Baghdad airspace that was controlled by the US military. At the time, we were the only civil company flying over the no-fly zone in and out of Baghdad. It was 2004, a year after the invasion of March 19, 2003, when the United States and various coalition forces initiated war on Iraq based on the idea that Saddam Hussein was building weapons of mass destruction.

The first part of the flight was routine. On a clear day I could easily see the fences that marked the country border on the ground, even from FL220 (22,000 ft). The one on the Jordan side looked like a long straight line, while the one on the Iraqi side was crooked. It always made us chuckle. At that point, it was time to turn off all lights, change the transponder to the special code we received in the morning and go into radio silence. For the next hour or so, we were on our own. Before reaching the vicinity of Baghdad, we contacted the airport to ensure they were aware of our arrival. Once in awhile when a glitch in communication occurred and they weren't expecting us, the military would scramble a couple of F18 jets to identify us.

In November of the previous year, a DHL airbus cargo flight was struck by a surface-to-air missile causing serious damage to a wing and the loss of the hydraulic system. The crew had only just managed to land the plane by using differential engine thrust. Despite veering off the runway, they survived the crash. To minimize the risk of becoming the next target of insurgents, the Americans put a special procedure in place where we maintained an altitude of a minimum of eighteen thousand feet until we were over the centre of the dual runways.

After the two-hour flight, Control approved our descent, we set the power to idle, props moved forward, flaps and landing gear lowered, and the plane slowed down to prepare for landing. Bringing it into a turn of 45- to 60-degree bank, we were now in configuration of an emergency descent. The Rate of Descent Indicator often showed the maximum as we were descending quickly. I preferred to take only a 45-degree bank because it was more comfortable for the passengers and for me. At 60 degrees, the G forces would cause my arm to feel heavy while reaching for the radio to switch frequencies with the tower.

As we were spiralling down, I was on constant lookout for other aircraft. Sometimes we would find ourselves sharing the spiral path with three or four others. Some were descending while others were ascending. It was enough to make your head spin.

"I've got him in sight! Oh, wait, I lost him again. Shit, where is he?" I would say.

Fortunately, being a smaller aircraft, we were mostly on the inside of the circles made by larger cargo planes. And by making a long, tight turn all the way down, we stayed clear of their path.

At four thousand feet, I contacted the tower for landing clearance, and we landed soon after while still in a turn. The complete descent procedure from top to bottom was four minutes. On the ground, we required only a portion of the runway. Avoiding the far ends of the runway kept us as far out of reach as possible from anyone who might try to shoot from the perimeter of the airport fence. They could still strike the airport though, as the sight of a mortar hole left in a pillar of the terminal reminded us every day. There was also the sound of nearby explosions and black smoke covering the sky in many parts of the city. The invasion was far from "Mission Accomplished."

As soon as I received the final passenger manifest in the terminal, I started working on my weight and balance sheet. The first leg of the flight was complete, but with another three lying ahead of us, there wasn't much time to sit around for a tea break. Plus, with the ground shaking from nearby explosions, I didn't want to remain on the tarmac too long. Being in the secure area of the green zone didn't mean we were 100% safe. When the passengers were ready, I led them out of the building and onto the tarmac. As we walked to the aircraft, I could see smoke rising on the horizon. Small black helicopters with people manning machine guns lifted off. They weren't US military but contractors from Blackwater, a known private military company. Iraq would see a dramatic increase in this type of organization over the next few years. Blackwater was only one of them, but because of a specific event in 2007 when Iraqi civilians were killed in Nisour Square in Baghdad, Blackwater generally came to mind when discussing private security forces. They received more than their share of bad publicity, but in reality they were doing an amazing job of protection given the circumstances. They saved countless lives.

I admired that they risked their lives to protect others. They were not there to protect us, specifically, and were not affiliated with us, but I always felt a sense of security knowing they were in the air with their "little birds" flying around the city when it was time for us to leave again. One after the other, our three Beech1900Ds departed Baghdad in the same fashion we had arrived. We would gain altitude in a corkscrew until out of reach of potential missiles. It was always more nerve-racking on the climb as we went much slower than during the descent. However, it was also exciting from a pilot's point of view. Applying full power and rolling down the runway, as soon as the aircraft lifted from the ground, we would lower the nose and stay only metres off the ground while retracting the flaps and the landing gear. The spiral climb required full acceleration well before reaching the end of the runway. Then, remaining as close as possible to the central point of the airport, we would pull up in a tight turn gaining altitude quickly. The Beech 1900D, a nineteen-passenger pressurized twin-engine turboprop, is the most popular aircraft in its category and used by many regional airlines.

Just for the heck of it, once in a while we would buzz the tower while turning, posing for pictures shot by the guys in Control. Hey, we had to have some fun in the middle of this crazy war, right?! It was also a way to release tension.

One of the planes went directly to home base in Amman after the two-hour flight back, and their short day was over. The other two would continue on. One was scheduled to fly an hour north to Erbil in the Kurdistan Region, one of the oldest continuously inhabited cities in the world. I always hoped I'd have a chance to visit and explore this city. The ancient history is amazing, and I would have loved to see the architecture of the Citadel of Erbil, but I was never there long enough. The other Beech was scheduled to fly an hour south to Al-Basra where the British military controlled the airport.

At some point during our flight, the US controller handed us over to the British. All we had to do was switch to a different frequency and follow their directions. One day, we were kept on radar vector, maintaining the specific heading upon which we were requested to fly. Time passed by and we weren't asked to return on course to our destination. After a few long minutes, the captain and I thought this was odd; they should have called us back by then. Out initial attempt to reach the controller received no answer. For some reason, we had lost communication with Baghdad. Knowing that we were getting closer to a border we weren't supposed to cross, we called Basra.

"Turn right! Now! Turn right!" someone screamed over the mic.

Following their frantic direction, we immediately initiated a turn and within seconds we were back on track. Still concerned about what had happened and wondering what the consequences might be, we landed a half hour later in Basra. We wanted to know a little more and used the occasion to visit the guys in the control tower and the radar room at the same time. A man with a thick British accent granted our request and welcomed us with a friendly smile. He showed us an image on the radar screen that indicated where we were when we restored radio contact—right on the border with Iran! Not a good place to be. For some unknown reason, there had been miscommunication between the US and British controllers that day, and we got caught in the middle. Luckily it ended well, and we avoided a major international incident.

The risk in Erbil and Basra was less than in Baghdad, but we employed the same spiral procedure to get in and out of the airports. The perimeter of safety was also smaller around the single runway, so we had to take this into account. After more paperwork, both planes headed back to Baghdad again. Once there, it was time to refuel, pick up or drop off passengers and fill out paperwork. After an hour or so on the ground, we made the two-hour flight back to Amman for the night. We had a little time to enjoy the evening, and then it was time for bed. The next day, it would start all over again.

I would usually get a day off per week, but I occasionally had to fly ten days in a row to cover for a sick crew member or a staff shortage. Despite the obvious stress and risks of such work, I was happier than ever. The excitement and the adrenaline rush I experienced made me feel so alive, and my previous job behind a desk quickly became a distant souvenir. I was exactly where I was meant to be.

A few weeks later, a new Air Serv captain moved into my apartment building. Brad was from Australia. Fun and easy-going, he was pleasant company, and I felt a little less alone among the South African pilots. They were a great group of people, don't get me wrong, but having someone from my own company was better. We were paired as a crew, which was fine by me. I had a blast flying with him. I also learned a lot, as he was very experienced. On the few empty legs without passengers, he let me sit in the left seat, the captain position, which is where you have access to more switches and levers as well as where you can start the engines. Having the opportunity to go through the start-up procedure and run-up checks was good training.

In Basra, the temperature was so hot that there were days when we had to get clearance for take-off before even starting the engines.

The heat raised the oil temperature too high if the engines were running while not moving, so we had to keep rolling until we were airborne, otherwise the gauge would go into the red, over the limit.

Back home in Canada, Paul was taking care of the house and had started the major renovations. This meant tearing down the walls on the bottom floor, leaving only the bathroom and shower in the middle of a big empty space. When he finally realized that money for renovating would not fall out of the sky, he finally got a job outside aviation. When he was young, he had worked as a heavy equipment operator, so he found work of this kind in town, enabling him to live at home. He wanted me to return and be together again, but I didn't want to right away. I wasn't going to stop what I was doing again just for him—especially since I loved my job and was exactly where I was meant to be.

However, before he left, he made sure to say what he needed to say to ensure I would eventually return—something I had waited to hear for many years: "Next year, on our ten-year anniversary, we'll get married," he said. Of course, I was happy to hear this and could finally put a name to our relationship. For years, I didn't know how to introduce him or present myself with him. I wasn't his girlfriend anymore—we were past that—but we weren't married, so I wasn't his wife. Maybe his common-law! That sounded too weird. The idea of a wedding made me happy, although I knew it wouldn't be fancy. I was having the time of my life flying in a dangerous part of the world where most people wouldn't think of setting foot, so I was content for the time being.

Despite my desire to stay and finish my contract year, a phone call a few weeks later put an end to it. While visiting the office, a secretary offered me a phone and said, "It's for you." *Who would be calling me here? Nobody besides Paul knows that I'm here.*

"Hello?" I said.

"Hi Myriam! It's your mother," the voice on the other end said.

I was stunned. For a second I didn't know how to respond. It had been years since we talked, and the only communication we'd had since I immigrated to Canada was in the form of greeting cards for birthdays and Christmas. But even those had ended when I received a nasty letter from my father a couple of years back. In his eyes I was the only one at fault for the broken relationship with the family, and they had never done anything wrong. His words were always very strong and hurtful, and if I had kept trying to discuss it, I would have never found the strength to grow internally. Although I felt I was done with them, they nevertheless wanted to visit me—in Jordan.

"No way," I said. "I'm working and have no time for visitors."

I didn't want to see them and had nothing left to say, but they insisted. That situation, probably organized by Paul searching for a way to get me back home, was enough to force me to quit my dream job. A couple of weeks later I was on my way back to Canada. I was angry, miserable and disappointed with myself. I had let the ones who were supposed to love and support me control and ruin my life again. I needed to make changes, once and for all, to find peace and happiness. Some of these changes would occur soon enough, but I was back home in Canada for now.

Waiting for passengers on the tarmac of
Baghdad International Airport, 2004

Starting the spiral descent procedure over
Baghdad International Airport

CHAPTER 10

CAN I HAVE A REFUND?

When I returned from the Middle East, I found the first level of our new house completely empty except for the bathroom at its centre. With no bedroom, Paul had moved the bed into a corner of the living room. It was actually just a big open space with no walls and no doors between the entrance, kitchen, dining and living rooms. We began renovating, but quickly ran out of money. It felt more like living on a construction site than in a cozy home. The winter was cold, and the only way to warm up was to sit next to the fireplace. However, we couldn't run it 24/7 and, once the remaining wood had burned, the temperature dropped quickly, the cold seeping in through the huge windows. Getting up in the morning with the temperature at only a few degrees was difficult, and going downstairs for a quick shower was even worse.

I couldn't stay home and do nothing under these conditions, so I looked for a job in town. I was prepared to do anything. There wasn't much to do in the small town of Golden, but I was hired at Kicking Horse Mountain Resort, the local ski area on the other side of the valley. I worked as a customer service agent, most days behind the ticket counter windows selling day passes. I never thought people who were out to have fun and enjoy a day of skiing would complain so much!

"There's too much snow! I want a refund!"

"Not enough snow!"

"It's too icy, give me my money back!"

I wasn't enjoying making minimum wage, but at least I was working. It kept me busy and offered an opportunity to get out of the house and meet people.

During the summer, the skis were put away and the slopes were opened to mountain bikes. Tourists would also come to visit Boo, the grizzly bear who resided on the slopes. He had his own enclosure, and a team fed and took care of him. Since I didn't want to stay indoors behind a desk, I decided to switch from office clerk to lift operator. The ones working that job were mostly young people just out of school or working for the summer. It was a bit awkward for me at thirty-two, but I didn't care. I liked being outside breathing fresh mountain air and enjoying the magnificent view.

Two major events were approaching at the end of the summer: my Canadian citizenship ceremony and our wedding. After more paperwork and a written test on the geography, history and politics of Canada, I was no longer a landed immigrant but a citizen of Canada. I walked out of the office feeling a renewed sense of belonging.

The second big day arrived in November. Just as Paul had promised a year previous, we married. It wasn't a big wedding, just a simple ceremony held on the shore of a lake.

Paul was still working as a heavy equipment operator, but no longer for the company in town. He moved again and was employed by a company in Canmore. As it was too far to drive back and forth each day, he decided to leave home Monday mornings, rent a room at the hotel for the week and drive back home Friday night. His mom visited for a month around our wedding, so I thought he would take a few days off to spend time with her and show her the sights since it was her first visit to Canada. But he didn't. He left me alone with her and, being winter, there wasn't really much to do. Since I was also working, she ended up spending many boring days at our house; she was miserable and made sure I was too!

Once she left, I started to realize that it was time to improve my life. I wasn't happy, and being married didn't change anything. I decided to contact Air Serv again to ask if they had a position for me on one of their projects. The answer was "yes," and I was offered a three-month contract based in Kabul, Afghanistan. I was very excited and accepted. As it was just before Christmas, they requested that the offer be placed on hold until after the holiday season.

I waited patiently while working at the ski resort. The winter season had started, and I worked as a janitor. I would start every morning at six before anyone else arrived at the lodge to clean bathrooms, vacuum the dining area, mop and dust. Cleaning up after thousands of skiers was a big task, and I had to get the lodge ready before it opened at eight in the morning.

When I was done in the lower lodge, I would don my ski gear and, with skis in one hand and vacuum in the other, I would ride the gondola up to the top of the mountain and clean the upper lodge. Once again, I had to race to finish before the first skiers arrived at the summit. If I managed to finish my work on time, I had the privilege of making the first run of the day in the pristine powder.

That was a great fringe benefit of this job. I repeated the process over a ten-hour shift, four days a week: clean, go up, clean, ski down. In addition, being a full-time employee of the resort, I had a free season pass. On my days off, I hit the slopes.

Air Serv cancelled their original offer to me in late January because they didn't want to send a female pilot into Afghanistan. Instead, they offered me a full-year contract to fly out of Africa again.

"Hell yes!" I exclaimed and signed the contract.

I could either be sent to the Congo to fly a King Air or to Chad to fly a Twin Otter. They didn't yet know which one it would be, so we processed visas for both countries. I told them that, given the choice, I would prefer Chad. Learning to fly a Twin Otter, that awesome DHC-6, was a dream of mine. However, I agreed to go anywhere they needed me. I would be happy just to fly and return to Africa! I couldn't have asked for more and was very excited.

After giving notice to the ski resort, I worked my last two weeks while planning and organizing yet another departure. This time, I was not about to let anything—or anyone—sabotage it. I would return only on days off, which was two weeks every three months. Including travel days, I would spend ten days at home to recharge before heading back. The posting turned out to be on the Twin Otter in Chad, so I was thrilled!

A new adventure began. I made a quick stop in South Africa to renew my South African validation, but it wasn't required since the aircraft was registered in the US. We got the validation anyway just in case I might have to switch to the Congo, which required such certification. After attending a few weeks of seminars and a ground course on the systems of the Twin Otter, I arrived in Chad. It was early 2006, and I believed this was going to be the best year of my life!

PART TWO

THE DREAM IS ALIVE

CHAPTER 11

AFRICA, HERE I COME

I was based in Abéché, a small city on the east side of Chad. As I stepped out of the Beech 1900 that had brought me there, a wall of heat made me gasp for air. It was hot—very hot!—dry and dusty. The town was on the edge of the desert, and it felt like being in the Wild West. There were no paved roads and no streetlights. It was in the middle of nowhere and was nothing like I had imagined. But I already loved it, and my huge smile revealed my satisfaction.

I noticed soldiers walking around holding AK-47s and other weapons at the airport. Many seemed too young to be in fatigues, and one of them looked like he was no older than twelve. While they deny it, many African countries employ child soldiers. It was sad to see them robbed of their childhood in this way, not only sad but also scary. A kid with a weapon is unpredictable and, throughout my years of visiting this continent, I never felt comfortable with it.

After greeting the chief pilot and base manager, I was driven to the compound where I'd be living. On the way, they explained that the rebels were planning a coup and marching into the capital, N'Djamena, hence the increased military presence. We were also on stand-by for evacuation in case they attempted the coup. What a "Welcome to Chad"! I was hoping the rebels held off on the coup because I had just arrived! I didn't want to have to evacuate and find myself on my way back home just because a bunch of rebels had planned to take over the government. Come on! Let me have at least a taste of flying that Twin Otter onto bush airstrips, a dream I'd held for years.

Three pilots, including me, the engineer who maintained the plane and the base manager shared the crew house. It was a big four-bedroom house in the middle of the compound with a couple of other buildings around it that included an extra bedroom, office and storage. One of the rooms housed the spare parts for the plane. The mechanic had pretty much everything he needed to fix anything on the plane. A general from the Chadian military owned the house and, at the rental price of well over $4000 US/month, he could have built a castle! A tall fence topped with barbwire surrounded the house and supposedly formed a safe enclosure. I say that because months later, we heard that a neighbouring compound was robbed at night and the guard killed. The robber had climbed the wall using a ladder and a thick blanket to protect himself from the wire.

During the day, we had a cook, a maid and a guard at the gate. At night, an armed guard from a security company took over the watch. A cat, a dog, a big desert turtle and a monkey also shared our life in the compound. It was like having our own private zoo! Well, sometimes it was a zoo, especially at night. The cat was there mostly to keep the mice at bay. But either he wasn't doing his job very well or there were too many of them. At night, I could hear the rats running in the ceiling. I didn't really want to see them, they sounded big!

City power was turned on for only a few hours a night but often didn't work, so we had two generators, the main one and an older spare as a backup, to run everything in the house. However, it wasn't sufficient to run all the air conditioning. The one in my room was at the end of the line, and I quickly learned it hardly worked. The fan I had on the ceiling spun at such a low speed that it's slow "woosh, woosh, woosh" was laughable. However, I didn't laugh much when it came time to sleep. The thick brick walls kept the heat stored inside during the day, and with no means of cooling it down quickly, I had to lie half naked, sweating, with my arms hanging on each side of the cot. It was like a sauna most nights, so I found it nearly impossible to fall asleep.

My bathroom was just a cubical addition to the room. There was no door, no window, just a concrete floor with a sink, toilet and showerhead. Taking a shower meant water would soak the surroundings, that is, when there was enough pressure. We had no hot water, which was OK most of the time. But during the winter season, the water was cold enough to clench your teeth. "Ouch!" those first few seconds required jumping up and down just to keep warm. But I wasn't complaining; at least there was water this time of the year. After the rainy season from June to September, not a drop of precipitation would fall for months. By the time May rolled around, the underground water level had dropped so much, most of the wells were dry. Some days we would turn the tap and nothing happened. On these occasions, we did a daily run across town to fill up three barrels wherever we could find water. Returning to the compound, each of us received a bucket of water for showering, flushing the toilet and other bathroom use.

These conditions seem harsh, but I couldn't have been happier. My dream of combining the three passions of my life—flying, Africa and helping others—had come true. I was more than ready to sacrifice home, comfort and stability to realize that dream. What's the value of comfort anyway? Most would be surprised how easily human beings can adapt. Any conditions that are voluntarily incurred can become the norm if accepted willingly and with a purpose.

There was a lot of work to be done in the region, and the plane was flying every day but Sundays. Starting with a trip in the morning and a quick lunch break, which was generally a sandwich while refuelling, we left for a second trip in the afternoon. As there were three pilots, we could rotate two days on, one day off, and so on. Having an extra pilot was mostly to cover for whoever got sick, something that happened often.

My introduction to the Twin Otter was done quickly, simply and on the job. The chief pilot, who was based in Uganda but travelled once in a while to visit our base for checks, was there to sign me off on that plane. I simply went on a normally-scheduled passenger flight with him. At our first stop, we dropped off the passengers, even the ones on transit, and I did three take-offs and three landings. Then we returned to pick up the passengers for the rest of the flight, and the check was finished.

We were there because of the disaster in Darfur. The flight schedule took us either to the north side of Abéché or to the south along the Sudanese border. The population from this Sudanese region had fled the violence, and the refugee camps across the border in Chad were ballooning in population. The war in Darfur began in 2003 when rebel groups began fighting the government of Sudan, who they accused of ethnic cleansing against non-Arabs. Hundreds of thousands of civilians were killed, and President Omar al-Bashir was indicted for genocide and crimes against humanity.

But it wasn't only about what was happening across the border. The events in Chad were more complex partly due to conflicts between tribes in local villages and, on a larger scale, the rebels against the government. The consequence was that, apart from the refugee camps filled with Sudanese fleeing Darfur, there was an increasing number of camps of IDPs, or Internally Displaced People. A Chadian seeking refuge in a camp because of the conflict in his or her own country was not a refugee but an IDP.

I was flying mainly on behalf of the United Nation Refugee Agency (UNHCR), but a number of seats on-board were allocated to other smaller humanitarian organizations. The plane was always filled to maximum capacity bringing personnel and supplies to the remote humanitarian camps spread along the border. We landed on three different airstrips on the north side. Bahai was the farthest, about a one-hour flight into the desert with miles and miles of sand all around. The runway, kept in good enough condition to land a plane, was simply a stretch of sand marked only with a line of small rocks along its edges. There were no other signs or markings. During the bad visibility days of the sandstorm season, the only way to find the runway was to line up on final approach using GPS, and we only knew where and when the threshold of the airstrip was reached when the headlights of two pickup trucks parked on each side of the runway appeared. Once we saw the lights, we knew we had arrived and, bringing the power back to idle, we awaited touchdown. The ground and sky were the same brown colour, and they blended together seamlessly.

We had to visit two airfields on our southern trip. They were hilly and green during the rainy season, and the challenge was to land on slick and muddy runways. Air service was vital to the people travelling with us since this was their only means of reaching these destinations. Most dirt roads were flooded, and movement on the ground was nearly impossible for these few months. Our Twin Otter was fitted with extra-large tires for good traction, however, once in a while we would still hydroplane either after landing or upon take-off, leaving me with an unpleasant feeling of losing control until we reached a patch of ground where traction was restored.

I quickly settled into my new life and, within a few days of flying, became comfortable with the DHC-6. I loved it all! The challenges were constant from every angle, either on the ground or in the air. Not one day was the same. By the end of the afternoon, we returned to our base and, after refuelling the plane and preparing for the next day, it was time to relax at the crew house before dinner. Some of us liked to settle on the couch with a laptop and on the internet. We were fortunate enough that our company installed a fairly good system. It worked well on most days, so much so that our compound often turned into an internet café for colleagues of other organizations.

We also had satellite TV, but I seldom used it. I didn't feel like sitting down after sitting all day in the cockpit, so I would usually drive around the corner to a French military base where I was allowed entry. It was a small outpost, their main base being in N'Djamena, but it was a safe haven for me where I was able to jog outdoors without constantly looking over my shoulder. I went running along the runway a few times, but I quit that the day a group of teenagers approached and started throwing stones at me. I gave up and remained inside the perimeter fence, running in circles. I have to admit that the additional view of military guys in short shorts was not an unpleasant sight! In return, I'm pretty sure they felt the same watching me run around their base. Ah yes, fringe benefits for everyone!

The French detachment was deployed there for four months. When their time expired, a new group would come in to replace the old. They had always been welcoming, and it became a habit for the departing team to introduce me to their replacements with a "Take good care of her, she's part of the family here." I met some great people there, and some became great friends I would see later in France.

I was often invited in for a drink after my daily run, and the conversation was always interesting. There were lots of drinking parties, many happening in our own compound, as most of the humanitarian workers were quite young. I never felt overly comfortable at these gatherings, but I fit in well on the military base, and it became like a second home. It was also a good way for me to remain current with the security situation in the area by exchanging information. They briefed me, at least with whatever they were allowed to, and in exchange, I would let them know if I'd seen anything out of the ordinary while flying around the region.

At the end of my first three months, it was time for a break. I packed a bag, boarded the Beech 1900 for N'Djamena and started the long journey back to Canada. A few days later, Paul picked me up in Calgary, and we drove the four hours home through the Rockies. The greenery was striking, and the mountains in all their beauty were amazing; I filled my lungs with deep breaths of fresh air. It was good to be home for a few days and nice to see him again. We'd been exchanging emails almost daily, and when the internet connection was good enough for a Skype call we had done that. But there was no denying that living so far away from each other in such different worlds was changing our relationship. I felt more distant. He had started a new flying job based in Calgary, but he was on a rotational schedule in and out of the great north. He seemed to like it, and we were both happy with our jobs. Ten days at home came and went and, after filling a suitcase with goodies I couldn't find in Chad, we said goodbye and I began my two-day trip back.

It was the beginning of the rainy season in Chad, so the mornings were beautiful for flying with blue skies and smooth air. But by the end of the morning, small puffy clouds appeared and grew larger within a few hours, which required us to manoeuvre around impressive thunderstorms. The afternoon flights became challenging as the rain had already started in the south. With no weather information other than looking up to scan the horizon, we never knew what conditions we would encounter at our destination. Some days, we were able to reach an airfield in fairly good weather, but by the time we turned around, a storm had matured, and we needed to fly miles out of our way to get home.

One of the refugee camps was located in the town of Goz Beida. It had a long runway, luckily so because after a heavy rainfall, a pool of water would cover part of the runway, rendering about a third of it unusable. Another camp was located in Koukou Angarana, a six-minute flight that would have taken at least an hour by car. The roads were flooded during the rainy season, so the inhabitants were cut off from everything. Everyone depended on the Twin Otter to get in or out. We sometimes did three or four quick trips between Goz Beida and Koukou. Once airborne, we cruised at one thousand feet, running quickly through the after take-off checklist, cruise checks, descent and approach and final checks, just in time to land again. Not much time to even breathe.

The Koukou airstrip was challenging, especially when wet. The runway was supposedly eight hundred metres long, though not all of it was usable. The village and the river were at one end, and a line of tall trees stood at the other, so we had little room for error. The surface often turned into thick mud when wet. Stepping out of the plane and onto its surface, we often sank to our ankles in the sticky mixture. Every time we arrived, the village kids would gather around the plane to see if we had anything for them. Sometimes it was just empty water bottles, which was what they sought most of the time. Sometimes we brought a bag of candy.

Leaving that airstrip was often nerve wracking. We were loaded to maximum weight, lined up to use every possible foot of the extremely short runway, and the flaps were set to twenty degrees, a configuration normally only used for landing. We used it there to allow the plane to get airborne quicker and at a slower speed than we normally would. It also necessitated keeping the control column as much aft as possible to release the front wheel from the mud. As soon as the plane lifted off, we lowered the nose to stay in ground effect, and retracted the flaps to ten degrees. Then we accelerated to start climbing before reaching the end of the runway and avoiding the trees in our path.

At the end of one work day back in Abéché, we spotted dark clouds rolling in from the porch of our home. Water! The first rains had finally begun and, to celebrate this first downpour, we donned our swimsuits and stood under the edge of the roof with water cascading over our heads. It was the best shower I've ever had!

One Saturday in the midst of an evening party with a group of friends visiting our compound, a call came in with a request for an immediate medevac (medical evacuation). Without knowing the details, everyone dropped what they were doing and prepared. Within thirty minutes, the plane and pilots were standing-by for departure. We never flew at night simply because the runway was not fitted for night flights and there were no lights at this airport. But when it became a matter of life or death, we had to do whatever it took. A few trucks parked along the edge of the strip to illuminate the runway with their headlights would generally do the trick.

While waiting for the patients to arrive, we received more details of what had happened. Two Spanish women who were working for different NGOs were planning to drive to another compound to join a team. One of them wanted to stop at her house to retrieve something and, to expedite things, instead of opening the gate to enter while in the car, she stepped out and walked into the compound. Meanwhile, her friend turned the truck around in preparation for a quick departure. While she waited, a man approached the side of the vehicle and, without a word, shot her twice. He opened the door and dragged her out, leaving her bleeding to death on the street. He jumped in their vehicle and drove away.

The victim was quickly transferred to the French military team and admitted to the infirmary on the base. Because this was a very limited facility, there wasn't much they could do except stabilize her. She needed to be evacuated to their main base in N'Djamena for emergency surgery, which was our responsibility. The French medical team boarded the rear of the Twin Otter with the patient on a mattress. During the two-and-a-half-hour flight to N'Djamena, they worked constantly to keep her alive as she was losing a lot of blood. Luckily, she survived and, after they had done everything they could in Chad, she was flown back to Europe where she received extensive medical care, leading to a full recovery.

A night curfew was implemented after that, and all social life was curtailed. Everyone stayed put, and movement outside after dark decreased to a minimum, especially for those located in the centre of town. Living right next to the airport, I was still able to take a quick ride around the corner to join friends at the base though. When I left for home at night, they would keep an eye on me until I had returned safely.

Being on stand-by for medevac was a big part of our job. Strangely, these flights almost always happened on weekends. We were usually called out to one of the airstrips to pick up sick or injured local patients. One of them was a ten-year-old boy who had picked up a landmine while playing in the bush. The explosion tore off both hands and part of one arm. The medics wrapped him in bandages, and we flew him directly to the capital in our Twin Otter for immediate care. His father at his side was crying, but the kid didn't make a sound. We were asked to return to N'Djamena to pick up the patient and his father a few weeks later, and we were relieved and happy to see that the son had survived. He wore a bright smile on his face while his father thanked us for saving the life of his only son. Moments like this gave us a great sense of accomplishment. I didn't always agree with some of the actions of humanitarian organizations—I saw money being wasted or misused—but it was worth it to save lives.

CHAPTER 12

SURGERY

Every so often, one of the team would get sick due to contaminated water or food. In such cases, diarrhoea would keep us down for a day or two. I'd been pretty lucky and hadn't had many issues with my health, but that was about to change.

I had stomach cramps one day, so I remained home and close to the bathroom. After a few days, I was back on my feet and in the cockpit, but it wasn't long before the cramps started again. This happened a few times before I realized that something was wrong. Instead of continuing the mild self-medication, I went to the infirmary at the French base, the only place in Abéché where expatriates could receive proper, though limited, health care. I felt they would be able to help with most basic problems and, if not, could recommend what to do next.

The nurse gave me antibiotics, and I rested for a few days. As the symptoms seemed to get better, I returned to work. But the stomach pain and fever returned. The worst bout occurred while in flight. We had spent the weekend in N'Djamena while servicing the aircraft and stocking up on goods unavailable in Abéché. On the return flight, I started feeling pain, which worsened over time. Luckily, there were two pilots on-board because it got so bad that all I could do was sit and concentrate on breathing. The pain felt like a truck running over my body. *What's going on?* I thought.

Upon returning to the base, I had a high fever and my skin was turning yellow, so I quickly went to the infirmary. Without a proper way to diagnose it, all the nurse could think of was either a liver infection or possibly appendicitis. He suggested I evacuate immediately for a proper examination, so I called my boss and explained the situation. Without thinking twice, they booked me a ticket back to Canada for that same evening. A couple of hours later, I was on-board a Beech 1900 that returned me to N'Djamena where I boarded my long flight out of Africa.

They notified Paul, and he made an appointment with my doctor in town for the next day for tests. Awaiting the results for the following twenty-four hours resulted in all sorts of ideas running through my head. When the phone finally rang, I was told to see the doctor at her office. That didn't sound good. It surely meant there was something wrong, otherwise she wouldn't have asked me to come to the office. An hour later, I was sitting nervously in her waiting room. She walked in and said, "So, here's your problem. No big deal, nothing dangerous, but you're going to need surgery."

My head was spinning as all I wanted was to fly back to Chad and get on with my life. I didn't want to be here!

"You have a gall stone about a centimetre wide, soft and moving around. When it blocks the duct passage, that's when you feel the pain," she explained.

The only way to get rid of it, she said, was to surgically remove the gall bladder. However, because it wasn't an immediate life-threatening condition, I was placed on a stand-by list for surgery. Health care in Canada is good but far from perfect. Due to long waiting lists, it sometimes takes weeks or months—if not years—to receive certain treatments.

What should I do in the meantime? Go back to Africa and continue my work knowing that once in a while the condition would act up and I would have to endure the pain? Before deciding anything, I had to talk to my aviation doctor. As a pilot, I had to pass a medical exam once a year to ensure flying fitness, and when something went wrong, I had to let them know. I booked an appointment and discussed my condition. It turned out that because it was symptomatic, my flight certification had to be suspended. Once I had the surgery, I could return for a new medical exam to re-qualify for certification. *Nooooo!!* I couldn't believe this was happening to me. Why? Why now? Why this? All I wanted was to return to my job.

I needed to find another solution and, thinking hard, I found one. Fortunately, I had full medical benefits through my company in the US, so I called them and discussed the situation. They said I should drive the two hours into the States to a city where the surgery could be performed within a week. With this option in mind, I called my doctor and explained what the aviation doctor had told me. I was ready to do it if she couldn't get me into a hospital in Alberta within the same time frame.

"You're not going to drive to the US for this, are you?"

"Oh yes I will!" I said.

"OK," she said, "Wait. Give me until tonight before making your decision. I'll see what I can do and get back to you before the end of day."

I patiently waited out the afternoon, stewing about the fact that they needed me in Abéché. There was so much work to be done, and the pilots were flying every day without a break in my absence. At five in the afternoon, the phone rang. When I picked it up, the doctor said, "I have you booked in the Canmore Hospital for Tuesday morning at eight. Because it's on short notice, the surgeon won't be able to meet you for a pre-surgery appointment, as is usually prescribed, so he'll do this the same day, prior to the operation. Have a good rest this weekend, and I'll see you after it's completed."

A few days later, I walked into the hospital and the surgeon assessed me. After being prepared for the operation, the anaesthetist told me to think of something nice. Well, I didn't have time to think—I was out like a light.

"Open your eyes! Open your eyes, it's over," said a voice.

The clock on the wall read 3:00 p.m., and my vision was very blurry. *Gosh, what's going on! Oh, yeah! That's right. I'm in the hospital and had surgery.* Oh, I felt like shit!

"Hey! How are you feeling?" Paul, who was sitting next to me, asked.

Where am I? Oh, yeah, that's right. I'm in a room now. Why am I having such a hard time waking up! I need to sleep. Let me sleep some more, I thought.

"You can be discharged and go home soon," said the nurse. "How's the pain? Do you need medication?"

It was a long three-hour ride back home, grimacing every time we hit a bump. My body awoke on the way, and the pain increased.

Paul was due to report back to work two days later, so he left me home alone rather than requesting time off to help out. As I watched him leave, I wasn't happy. Maybe we were growing apart because we were living so far away from each other. Or maybe it was because living on my own and doing things I had always wanted to do opened my eyes to what I had been missing. I wasn't sure, but something was definitely different. As I was still mostly lying down to recuperate, he packed his bag knowing that I'd probably leave before he returned.

When the surgeon asked when I planned to go back to Africa, I told him I'd like to leave in two weeks. He advised me to take a month off to rest after surgery, so I reluctantly compromised on three weeks. Before Paul left that morning, I asked him to at least bring in a pile of wood from the shed and stack it up next to the fireplace. I wasn't allowed to carry anything heavy for a couple of months and, even more so, right after surgery. He did so and, after a goodbye kiss, left. Gosh, I was bored sitting in a big house with nothing to do. There was so much I could do in Africa. All I could think of was what I was missing: the flying, friends, jogging, laughter, risks, heat, smells, everything!

I had been home alone for ten days and was feeling much better, though my stomach muscles were still sore. It was a bright, sunny day, and I needed to do something because I thought I would lose my mind just sitting around and waiting another ten days to fly out. I decided the windows needed cleaning. There were a lot of windows in that house and basically a huge wall of glass on the south side! The only way I could reach the second story on the outside was by using an extension pole. Holding it above my head to reach the top portion required contorting my body to avoid putting too much pressure on my stomach muscles, but I managed and, a few hours later, happy with a job well done, I laid down on the couch for a break.

As I got up and headed to the kitchen an hour later, I felt a sharp pain extending from the bottom of my back and shooting through the length of it. *Now what's going on?* I thought. The pain pinned me down, and I screamed when I tried to move again. I couldn't move! It hurt so much that tears rolled down my cheeks. Very slowly, I managed to roll down on the floor and drag myself onto the bed a few metres away. I stayed there for the rest of the night, not even hungry anymore. I hoped that after a good night's sleep, it would improve, but it was a long night. Every movement sent shock waves through my body. *What have I done?*

The next morning, I called the doctor's office, but she wasn't working that day. It was Friday, so I had to wait until after the weekend, but I was determined to find help. I grabbed the phone book and decided to call a physiotherapist. Luckily, I got an answer and, after explaining my situation, was advised to come in right away.

I first had to get into the Jeep and drive thirteen kilometres into town. I moved as slowly as I could to avoid the shooting pain, and I finally arrived. Upon seeing me struggle to get out of the car, the physio came out and helped me walk to her office. After an hour of treatment, I wasn't perfect but at least most of the pain was relieved. Stupid me; that was the consequence for not resting when I should have. The physiotherapist suggested I return the next day, so I went home promising myself to not do anything stupid anymore.

As I was walking in, the phone rang. It was Air Serv. Something had happened in Abéché and they needed me back sooner if I was

OK to travel. They wanted me to leave Sunday—in two days! It must have been some kind of emergency for them to ask with such short notice. I didn't want to tell them about re-injuring myself and the shape I was in, so I said I would leave earlier, but not before the following Wednesday. Sunday was just too soon. I needed at least a few more sessions with the physiotherapist to enable me to sit on the long flight to Africa. I had three more days to get back on my feet in sufficient shape for the cockpit. Wishful thinking, but I was determined to make it work.

A week later, I was back on the dusty ground of Abéché. They needed me so urgently because one of the other pilots had taken time off to go home and resolve important personal matters. Anyway, the operation couldn't just stop for two full weeks until I returned. So, I quickly refocused on work and started flying again. I was happy to be back at it. *Sorry, Doctor*, I thought. He'd probably be pretty angry if he knew I was flying again. But I was OK now. I promised myself not to lift heavy bags for at least a month, and the rest of my team made sure I didn't.

A new team had arrived at the military base, so I didn't have a chance to say goodbye to and thank the nurse who helped me. I wrote him a message later, letting him know what had happened and that I was doing well and back at work.

CHAPTER 13

REBELS ATTACK

I was up early on a Saturday morning a few weeks later. We had a flight to the north in the morning, and our base manager had already left for the airport to supervise the handling of check-ins and cargo distribution. As I walked out of my room, I heard a strange noise—almost like fireworks mixed with someone hitting a brick wall. The sound was sharp and sporadic. I walked out on to the porch to listen; it seemed to be coming from a distance. Our Ugandan engineer, Tony, came out to the porch too. As a child, Tony had been abducted by the Lord's Resistance Army (LRA), led by the infamous Kony, and forced to become a soldier. Burn scars on his forearms were evidence of the horrors he must have endured. The noises in the distance made him nervous—he knew the sound of shooting when he heard it. And it wasn't just a couple of shots like we were used to hearing. It sounded like heavy fighting. Everyone in camp could now differentiate the small arms from the heavy calibre fire and explosions.

Steve, the other pilot, marched out of his room still half asleep after a late party the night before and shouted, "Who's banging against the wall at six in the morning?"

"Man! Nothing is happening here," Tony said, "but there's something going seriously wrong not far from us!"

The sound of the heavy fighting was getting closer as the battle reached the edge of town. It lasted for two hours before all fell silent. The humanitarian community, linked by handheld radios, were listening on the same channel to someone from the UNHCR communicating the latest news and advice. For now, the orders were to stay put and not leave our compounds. The rebels were roaming the streets and had taken over the town. We could see them passing in front of our gate, which was freaky because we had no idea what they were up to or their intentions toward us. We spent the rest of the day discussing our options. Should we stay put and see what will happen? Should we pack up, load the aircraft and fly to N'Djamena where we could stay at our country manager's residence? The aircraft would be more secure at the international airport. We would also be on site if evacuating the country became a necessity. We spent the next few hours reviewing different scenarios and waiting next to the radio for directives.

It was a long day, and the eerie silence after the fighting was getting to us. The radio crackled and we finally heard the voice of the UNHCR chief. We were told that although the town was under rebel control, they had nothing against the expatriate community. For safety reasons, we were asked to drive to the French military base to seek refuge for the night. We had to move before nightfall, which was quickly approaching, but the base was just around the corner, so it was a quick drive. Others were on the opposite side of town and had to organize a convoy to safely drive through the empty streets.

We gathered a few essential items: passport, personal computer and a change of clothing, and were ready in a few minutes. We also packed extra food and water, as we were requested to bring what we could to help. The base wasn't equipped to feed an additional 150 people, though they could provide beds or cots, indoors and out. The guys took the car and I jumped in the pickup. We didn't lock any doors because some of our local staff decided to remain in the compound to watch over the house. We knew that if someone decided to ransack our compound, opposing them would bring a worse outcome than just letting them in. It wasn't worth trading a life for household stuff.

We drove around the corner to find ourselves in a long line of vehicles waiting to pass through security before entering the base. The military was in full battle gear. The relaxed atmosphere I was used to there after a day's work was gone, and the uncertainty of the events was stressing out many expatriates.

The French were good at settling us. Once everyone was inside and the gate closed for the night, we gathered for a meeting. We had been invited here, but that didn't mean we could do whatever we wanted. Once everyone understood the rules and where we were allowed to access, we claimed a cot for the night and gathered around the table for a quiet dinner. People were responding differently to what had happened that day. Some were fairly relaxed, and others were still afraid. A few French soldiers remained behind to discuss, help or answer any questions we might have in order to calm the ones who needed it. One of them, Daniel, was put in charge of looking after the needs of all the expatriates in the camp.

I was doing fine, not stressed or scared. In fact, I was more excited than anything. I've always been drawn to risks, danger and action. The adrenaline rushing through my veins made me feel alive, and my addiction has only increased over the years. The lows between adventures became deeper. Most people didn't understand why, and that was OK. I've never sought understanding of this need to put myself in risky situations, but I always hoped for acceptance, although it was difficult to find.

For the time being, I was in the thick of the action and needed to get some sleep. I snuck under the walls of my cot, which resembled a little tent on the bed. It provided protection against mosquitoes and privacy from others lying a few feet away. I was sleeping indoors. Some of the cots had been installed in a large room where military personnel gathered to watch TV or play pool, and it was decided that only women would sleep there. I didn't sleep all night because of the noise! Who says women don't snore? I kept tossing and turning, waiting for morning to arrive.

Once everyone awoke, another meeting was organized to update the situation before breakfast. For the time being, no one could leave the safety of the camp, so we settled in for a long day of sitting around and doing nothing. We weren't happy about it, especially since our house was just around the corner and all our belongings were there. But we didn't have a choice, so we made the most of it. Expatriates who hadn't made it in the night before arrived. There was also talk of evacuating all unnecessary staff to N'Djamena and eventually back to their home countries. This being the case, I knew there were many expatriates still working in the refugee camps who needed a way out too.

I spoke with Steve about sending our Twin Otter to retrieve these people so they could access a French military aircraft, the Transall, to shuttle them from Abéché to N'Djamena. I really believed we should be helping and doing something instead of just sitting around and waiting. We had the aircraft and were there to save lives, after all. It was our responsibility!

After completing a risk assessment, we agreed we should do it, so we discussed it by phone with our country director in N'Djamena.

As he contemplated our idea, the sun went down and we prepared for a second night of camping. This time, I decided to move out of the "ladies room" and joined the rest of my team in one of the outdoor areas. I finally managed to fall asleep late that night once everyone had settled in.

I woke up shivering around two in the morning. The temperature had dropped overnight, and with few blankets or pillows and no coat, I was cold. Very cold! The rest of the night once again involved waiting to finally see the sun rise and heat the earth. When morning finally arrived, it was a replica of the previous day: a meeting, breakfast, and sitting around and waiting.

Our director called to check on how we were doing and to boost our spirits. We discussed the evacuation plan and, with the support of our headquarters in the US, it was up to him to seek the approval of the French military that controlled the airport and surrounding area. At first, they were surprised about our proposal and our willingness to take the risk. But in the end, they agreed and gave the go ahead for the operation. We would work with them to co-ordinate the flights and ensure safety for all concerned. Knowing that the rebels were still in town, Steve and I devised a special procedure for departures and landings that helped keep us out of reach of possible shooting. I was basically taking the spiral procedure I used in Iraq and applying it in accordance with the structural limits of the Twin Otter.

With permission to proceed, we planned our first flight for the afternoon. But beforehand, we needed to return to our house for documents, headsets, uniforms and other essential items. Even though the house was just a few minutes away, the French were very nervous, and they didn't want to let me go alone. Steve joined me and we jumped in the pickup ready to go. Before they opened the gate for us, a soldier said, "Don't worry! We'll have our eyes on you all the way. Just drive and don't stop 'til you get there. Make it quick, gather what you need and come back right away." Steve and I looked at each other, and with an "OK!" we drove away.

As we rounded the first curve along the wall of the base, I saw a gathering of pickups with Chadians in various camouflage uniforms. I realized immediately that they weren't local militia but rebels. My heart was pounding, and I scanned the group for any potential threat as I drove past. At first, I was surprised that they hadn't tried to stop us. How was I to know they had spoken to the French military earlier that morning about our intentions? They said they weren't directly interested in us, though you never know what goes through their minds when under the influence of drugs. They use Khat, a plant commonly found in eastern Africa. Chewing the leaves gave them energy, reduced hunger and made them euphoric.

We picked up what we needed along with extra clothing, blankets and pillows as well as some items for our teammates. We quickly piled everything in the back of the truck and returned to the base. When we received a "Welcome back" from security, I almost wanted to rip his head off for not warning us about the rebels, but I realized they didn't want to alarm the expats in the compound. I smiled back and told Steve we should probably not discuss what we had just seen.

We prepared our aircraft under the watchful eyes of the French military securing the runway. While we waited for the fuel truck to finish filling up our tanks, the UNHCR security officer briefed us on the situation at the camps we were heading to. It was only when we entered the runway and rolled to the end of it to place ourselves in take-off position that we noticed how many troops the French military had deployed to secure the perimeter. I have no doubt that for each machine gun we saw, there were more hidden farther away in the bush. With a mixture of stress and confidence, we took off toward the north.

Once in the air, it was just like any other flight. We stopped at a few usual destinations and picked up as many people as we could before heading back to base before the end of afternoon. Meanwhile, the French had started their own evacuation, and their first load of people was lined up waiting to board the flight out of Abéché. At the end of day, another update meeting revealed that we would probably be staying at the French base for the remainder of the week.

Knowing that we would now be flying every day, Daniel kindly offered Steve and I one of the extra rooms instead of the cots outside. It was very generous, even if it was just a container room with enough space for two beds. We were still happy to have a bed in a quiet, warm place to get the rest we needed for another day in the cockpit.

After a refreshing shower in the communal washroom, I put on fresh clothing and joined the team for dinner. We spent a relaxing evening with drinks and conversation under a bright sky full of stars. The next few days, we helped evacuate all non-essential expatriate staff. The rebels had only taken over Abéché to show what they were capable of, but their goal was to keep going west until they reached the capital. By day four, they had left the town but were still in the surrounding area and, for safety reasons, the French military didn't let us return home quite yet.

We flew south that afternoon, and even though we were still sleeping at the base, the days had begun to normalize. While in flight, we were still on alert just in case we spied a column of suspicious trucks. All looked fine as we approached Goz Beida, so we descended to establish a final approach to the airstrip. After a smooth landing, we rolled onto the tarmac, shut down the engines and opened the door for the passengers to exit. Suddenly I heard a strange noise. *What the heck?* I looked in the direction of the sound to see one of the tires deflating so fast that the plane leaned to one side. What a sad sight our plane was with its left wing tip pointing to the ground. Our tires were getting worn out by extended use on dirt and rocky strips, and we must have hit a pretty sharp stone because there was a large cut in the tire. What now?

We tried to contact our mechanic back at the base but, because of the recent events, cell phone lines in Abéché were still down. Luckily for us that day, a second aircraft was back in the air. A Cessna Caravan from Médecins Sans Frontières (MSF) had joined the evacuation effort and landed just a few minutes behind us. They were supposed to continue on to another strip in the south, but the pilots, despite being under pressure to finish their scheduled trip, refused to leave us stranded. They knew there were rebels in the area that made it unsafe to stay on the ground very long in Goz Beida. They got airborne right away and returned to Abéché to pick up our engineer, a spare tire and the tools required to change it in the field.

They were back a few hours later, and our mechanic got to work. A truck from UNHCR came from the refugee camp with a compressor to inflate the new tire and, soon enough, we were back in business. When we landed back at base at the end of that day, a group of French soldiers came to check on us as we parked the plane. They were worried and thought we had been caught in the line of fire. After explaining what had happened, everyone relaxed. Shit always happens at the wrong time and place. In the end, all was fine, and no one was hurt.

I made some good friends that week. People come together in hard times because everyone needs to depend on others. Steve began dating a girl he met that week who worked for a small NGO, and they married and had two children. It's funny but during those last few days, several couples formed and new friendships began. I was no exception.

After a week at the base, we were finally allowed to go back to our own compound. Most of the expatriates had been evacuated by then, and the remaining community was quite small. We were happy to return to our normal lives. We were also eager to see if our house was still standing and if we had been robbed during the previous few days. As we opened the gate and rolled in, everything was as we had left it. We happily resettled back into our own rooms. What a relief!

As our lives returned to normal over the next few weeks, I spent more time at the French military base, and I became close friends with Daniel. I had always felt comfortable at the base, but now I felt even more at home with the military than with my own crew. I would join them for early morning runway runs on Sundays, sports, drinks, dinner or just to sit and talk in their offices. They would even pick me up and drive into town for an evening out at a local restaurant. I was really having the time of my life!

CHAPTER 14

MOVING ON

With everything that had happened the previous few weeks and months, I began to question my life with Paul. We were still in touch, but conversations were brief. Our relationship made less and less sense, and experiencing the life I had been missing for years opened my eyes. I was not even able to say "I love you" to him anymore. It felt like a lie, and he knew it. He had noticed the change and was preparing for the inevitable. We didn't talk about it much over the phone or in writing, but I nevertheless knew deep inside what I had to do the next time I was at home.

I was due to return to Canada in February for a month off at the end of my yearly contract. To many of my colleagues' surprise, I signed to extend my contract. No one thought I'd last a whole year let alone sign up for a second. In fact, until I came along, no one had ever completed a full year. The harsh conditions and the difficulty of the work caused most employees to quit after a few months. But I loved it and the challenges. I was flying and saving lives. I was doing exactly what I had always wanted to do. It was perfect, and I was exactly where I was meant to be.

In December 2006, I was enjoying the fair weather and great days of flying. Christmas and New Years were coming, and I was excited because I wasn't going to spend Christmas alone or bored at home for once. All the expatriates in town were invited to a banquet at the French military base. They had moved the aircraft and helicopters out of the hanger and replaced them with rows of tables on the tarmac. Military personnel and civilians mixed, and it was a fun night of good food, drinks, music, dance and comical shows. It was a night where everyone could forget the horrid conditions, danger, the sadness of the refugee camps and IDPs, the conflict between villages, clans, rebels and militia, and the difficult lives of the locals.

It was getting late, and everyone had drank too much. The French soldiers had to shut down the party, but Daniel didn't want to let me go. As a civilian, I was supposed to leave the base, but he decided to sneak out of the base and escort me back to my crew house. What occurred next was inevitable. I had tried to push my feelings away because I was still married, but I couldn't fight them anymore. With the growing feelings Daniel and I had for each other, it was only a matter of time.

I felt ashamed, like the worst person on Earth, for the next few days. I had cheated. This wasn't me. How could I have done this? However, as soon as I saw Daniel again, I knew that the life I was sharing with Paul wasn't right; it never had been. Yes, it was wrong to cheat, but it wasn't like we were living under the same roof anymore. We had been apart for so long, not only physically. We were already living our own lives, each never really knowing what the other was doing. Like everyone else, I needed love and comfort and couldn't recall when I last had those feelings. I wasn't trying to find excuses for my wrongdoing, but I had woken up to the fact that our separation was going to happen sooner or later. Years of resentment had built up every time I had put myself and my needs aside. Now more than ever, I knew what I had to do. But I didn't want to do it from a distance; I'd be returning home in a couple of weeks. It was going to be difficult—the hardest thing I'd ever done in my life—but it had to be done. For me and for Paul.

I was by myself the first few days in Canada as Paul was still working up north. When he returned, I picked him up at the Greyhound bus depot. I was feeling sick to my stomach and my hands were shaking. When he walked out of the bus, we looked at each other and both forced a smile. He knew as well as I did what was coming next. He wanted to start the conversation while driving home, but I preferred to wait until we arrived.

We had a quiet conversation, no raised voices, no big drama, but we were both crying. Strangely, it was like we were already prepared for this and were just waiting for it to happen. Though he asked me not to leave, he didn't try very hard to stop me. We spent those next few days together at home, sharing things like we used to. He slept on one side of the bed and I on the other. It was just like old friends spending a few days together. We cried and talked about it more and, when the time came for each of us to return to work, we packed our bags and returned to our own separate lives.

I received an email from him a few days after returning to Chad. He reviewed the previous twelve years, outlining when he should have done or said something but hadn't. He listed all the important moments when I had needed him to understand and help me. That letter made me angry because he admitted how consciously selfish he had been. Each time I thought he hadn't realized how much he was hurting me, he had actually known and remembered. My heart broke into pieces, and I cried until I had no more tears.

CHAPTER 15

HOW MANY GUNS?

I didn't have much time to think about my personal life because there was too much going on in eastern Chad. A pilot had left and a new one arrived. While I was busy showing him the ropes, there was yet another conflict between two villages around Guéréda. There were multiple wounded people who needed immediate evacuation, and we were called upon to do it. Within ten minutes, I was in my uniform and on my way to the aircraft. I filed a flight plan, quickly checked the weather—which was pretty much a scan of the horizon—and we were airborne in less than thirty minutes. We arrived at our destination half an hour later with security waiting for us on the strip. We gathered as much information as we could about the patients' conditions and organized the cabin to suit their needs. We were told that two of them could sit and three would be on mattresses, all suffering multiple gunshot wounds. We quickly unclipped the number of seats we needed to accommodate them and folded them against the walls.

The Twin Otter was the perfect fit for these kinds of flights; there was no carpet, just metal flooring, making it easy to clean. After cargo flights full of mud or medevacs full of blood, trust me, you didn't want carpet. We also had a passenger door with only a simple ladder hooking at the bottom instead of the usual large doorstep, which made it easy to load or offload cargo or, in this instance, to slide a patient in or out on a stretcher or a mattress. We had to do with what we had in these instances. No fancy equipment.

When the ambulance arrived, we loaded the wounded one by one, starting with the two who could sit in the forward cabin. Once everyone was on-board and secured, a doctor joined us, and we took off. We flew back to base, remaining as low as we could to avoid breathing problems for the patients, but high enough to avoid turbulence. Once in Abéché they were taken to the local hospital for rudimentary treatment. Considering what I'd heard about that hospital, if anything had ever happened to me, I wouldn't go there. They had next to nothing for medical treatment, no proper operating rooms, no supplies, and let's not talk about sanitation. As expatriates we were very fortunate to have access to the French military medical site, as well as the means of evacuation overseas if necessary.

At the end of a day like this we each had our own way to relax. Some just sat in their rooms talking on Skype with their loved ones back home. Others either watched TV or went outside on the porch with a drink and a book to admire the sunset. I still had too much energy, and the only way to burn it off was to change into my sports gear and head back to the French base for a good run. Strangely, I had never run much in my life, but I started doing so there. At the beginning, I was only able to do one or two laps around the base, about a kilometre or so, but eventually I increased the runs to seven or eight laps. Mind you, I ran in temperatures well over 30°C, so that's all most people could muster. It was my way of decompressing, and my body felt good after a day of sitting in the cockpit. The Twin Otter didn't have the most comfortable seats. Exercise was also a way of clearing my mind of the horrors we often observed.

There were also some enjoyable moments. One quiet Sunday there were no scheduled flights and no medical evacuations. The team decided to go on a camel ride, our guard having called a friend who owned camels. He was a nomad who was staying in a small village just outside of town. Early one morning, his men led the camels up to our gate. After putting on sunscreen, and with hat, glasses and water bottle in our packs, we gathered together feeling adventurous. The saddles were made of wood and cushioned with rugs. Some camels had beautiful ornaments on them and looked very proud. Everyone but our base manager chose a camel; he decided to ride a horse. Sitting as best we could while holding onto the front of the saddle, we managed not to fall over when the camels stood on their hind legs. We strolled out of town enjoying the fresh breeze of the morning and the cooler temperature.

The colours of the sand and small hills around us kept changing. It felt good to be out in the bush moving at a slow pace and enjoying the silence. Living with the constant noise of aircraft engines and generators at home, I had almost forgotten what it was like to experience nothing but quiet around me. I missed that. We had a break at a village where they had prepared hot tea for us, a welcome respite for our sore butts.

I noticed that some of the camels wore a metal loop above their foreheads that had nothing attached to it and wasn't part of the decoration. While sipping tea and conversing with the villagers, I asked one of them what it was.

"This is where you put the tip of your rifle so you can shoot while riding the camel," he said with jarring simplicity.

That brought me right back into the reality of life in Chad.

The sun was high above us and soon it would start burning our skin in the heat of midday, so it was time to ride home. It was the hottest, dustiest, driest season of the year. We arrived home after a few hours, everyone having enjoyed this nice break from the daily routine. After exchanging presents with the camel driver it was time for a thorough shower. We definitely needed one, and I think we all showered with our clothes on because they needed washing too. Camels don't smell like roses! It was also sandstorm season again, especially in the north, and visibility often went from bad to worse. Grains of sand stuck to sweat and made our skin feel like sandpaper.

One of the rules about flying in our aircraft was, "No guns." We were working on humanitarian missions, and a sticker on the side of the airplane door was self-explanatory: "No Arms On Board." As standard procedure, we checked the passengers with a hand-wand before allowing anyone on, and I always found it to be a bit of a diplomatic challenge to discuss it with passengers. Finding a way to convey the rules without upsetting them was often difficult and could easily and quickly lead to confrontation.

On one trip out of Goz Beida, the prefect of the town wanted a flight to Abéché, but he wasn't on our flight manifest and the plane was full. We did our best to make him understand that no matter who he was we weren't allowed to make changes without approval if he hadn't booked ahead. He wouldn't take "no" for an answer, and his entourage lifted their AK-47s and pointed them at us, demanding that we take him to Abéché.

"Welcome aboard!" I said.

We were hijacked. Some of our passengers remained behind to make room for the prefect. Of course, we filed a proper report, and I heard it went all the way to the office of the Chadian president, Idriss Déby, who handled the matter.

Soon after, I had a flight to Bahai scheduled to pick up a VIP with his escorts to be flown back to Abéché. I asked that they leave their guns behind if they had any before stepping on-board to be scanned. The male pilot scanned them one by one because I didn't want to overstep my boundaries as a female; it was a measure of respect. While this VIP was standing in his djellaba while holding his arms up to be checked, I heard a *bip* along his forearm. With a smile, he pulled out a knife and handed it to his driver. The wand continued and *biiiip* again! Sliding his hand under the fabric, he disclosed a rifle along his side.

"Nice!" I said with a smile.

He smiled back.

My partner then stepped in front of him and scanned his legs, *biiiip*. Really, you've got to be kidding! Lifting his djellaba, he pulled out a sawed-off shotgun attached to his ankle. I wanted everyone to remain calm and to keep the situation under control, so I kept smiling and jokingly said, "You have a whole arsenal on you!" He laughed, though the situation was still dangerous since others had overreacted in the past under these circumstances. He wanted to at least keep the shotgun with him, but I wasn't standing down on principle. He kept saying that it wasn't loaded, so there was no reason to be concerned.

Suddenly, he drew out the gun as if loading it. All I could hear was the sound of sand grinding in the metal. *krrrrrrrssshhh*. He raised it in front of my face and said, "Look, it's empty!"

"Holy shit! Get that thing away from me!" I shouted.

"No, but look, it's empty, no bullets!" he kept saying.

"I don't care! Put it away, I don't want to see it!" I replied.

Now I was angry. Everyone else froze, not knowing what to say or do. I looked at our passengers and simply said, "On board! Now! Without your guns! Or we leave without you. I'm the captain here, it's my flight, my rules, and nobody goes anywhere unless they agree." He just looked at me, said "OK!" and off we went. During the flight back I couldn't help wondering how that gun could work properly with so much sand in it anyways! Unbelievable!

Well, that was a story to tell that evening while relaxing with my friends at the French base. Daniel and I were enjoying every moment we could share and, even though we had no idea where the relationship would lead, we were just living in the moment. One evening after I had gone into town for dinner with him and three of his buddies, he wanted me to spend the night with him. Although visitors were not allowed in the base after hours, he was determined to sneak me in. The tricky part was getting past the front gate security without being seen. He decided to hide me in the car while passing the gate.

"Hi there," he said to the soldier taking names and license plate numbers. It was pitch black outside, and Daniel pretended the light inside the car was broken, so the soldier couldn't see me sprawled under the legs of the two people sitting in the back. We tried to remain serious until far enough from the gate to avoid being heard, then we laughed like teenagers.

Daniel ensured no one was guarding the hall leading to the rooms, and I sneaked into his room. One of the three "helpers" was actually the chief of security at the camp. He kept shaking his head, saying, "What are you doing to me!" I could still hear them laughing in the hallway.

Once in a while, we had special visitors from the US. When prominent people visited, I acted on behalf of the UNHCR. It was good publicity and a way of making people aware of the tragedy unfolding across the border in Darfur. I had the pleasure of meeting Angelina Jolie while flying from Abéché to one of the camps, and Mia Farrow on multiple occasions when she visited Chad. They were very humble and respectful, and I was amazed at the level of awareness they could raise by using their fame.

Aside from actresses, we sometimes flew delegations of politicians to visit refugee camps. I didn't particularly enjoy these flights because most of the time we waited next to the plane for hours until everyone decided to leave. We had to tag-along all day, or sit and wait in a corner until they finished their visit. We always had a planned schedule, but these VIP trips never followed it. As pilots we had to keep pushing everyone to end long goodbyes to ensure making it back before dark. If the sun went down, everyone on-board would get stuck out in the bush overnight because there were no lights on the airstrips for night flight.

One particular visit was particularly disgusting because it seemed like the political optics were more important than the horrors in the region. As the visitors walked into the refugee camp, the humanitarian staff arranged the kids in a circle, having them sing and put on a show as if in a circus. Most of them were probably wearing the only piece of clothing they owned and were walking around in bare feet. Part of the visitors' entourage included wives and close friends. One of them looked more like she was putting on a fashion show in New York than visiting a refugee camp in eastern Chad full of hungry people whose safety was in severe jeopardy after losing their homes. The excessive jewellery on her ears, around her neck and on each finger made me very uncomfortable. The value of her hardware alone must have been more than the sum of everything owned by every soul in that camp of thousands of refugees.

Before the next rainy season, we also busied ourselves packing to move into a new compound next door on the other side of the perimeter wall. Organizing a move in North America isn't too complicated, but it was challenging and frustrating in Chad while we had to continue flying to avoid disrupting scheduled flights. To enhance co-ordination, I let the two other pilots continue the flights so I could supervise the move on the ground. The fact that I was the only one fluent in French made it easier for me to handle those types of things. Together with our local staff, I went back and forth from one house to the other with truckloads of furniture, personal belongings and spare parts for the aircraft.

Once everything was moved around the corner, there were two remaining items that I didn't know how the hell to move: the generators. This was where having good relations with the French military on the base came in handy. After explaining the situation to my friends and obtaining their supervisor's approval, they came to my rescue with a forklift and a truck. After laying a concrete foundation at the new location, they picked up one generator at a time and delivered them to the new compound. And voila! Once again, I thanked the French forces for their great support. Gosh, I loved those guys! It might not seem like much, but simple things there mattered so much more than they do in a developed country.

A few weeks later, I had to say a final goodbye to this military team. Their four-month tour of duty had ended, and the base would once again see a rotation of new soldiers. Keeping busy with the move and the flying helped me forget about Daniel leaving.

Because of our deep feelings for each other, we weren't looking forward to this separation, but there was nothing we could do about it. We decided to keep in touch and hoped to find a way to see each other again in the future to reassess the relationship. As usual, the old team introduced me to their replacement, who in turn promised to take care of and watch over me.

CHAPTER 16

HORROR AND BEAUTY

Nearing the end of the dry season, I kept a watchful eye on the small clouds popping up here and there during our flights. The dry, hot air finally left, bringing more humidity. With that, flies became as annoying and aggressive as they could be in Africa. The fun of playing with the Twin Otter around the clouds soon turned to tricky flight planning and frightening thunderstorms resulting in challenging conditions. The rainy season had already begun in the south where airstrips dissolved into mud and pools of water after a storm.

While on a return flight from N'Djamena for a weekend of maintenance, Mother Nature graced us with an amazing sight. While cruising at ten thousand feet with dark clouds from a distant storm in front, we saw a wall of sand moving slowly in our direction. Rising high off the ground it made everything below disappear into a cloud of dust. It was like flying into a sandwich of darkness between sky and ground as the sand turned different shades of brown and grey. Although it was beautiful to watch, our stress mounted as we had to keep moving forward blindly and search for an opening through which to pass. That was the first time I'd ever seen this phenomenon called a Haboob.

My second experience was back at the house at the end of a regular day. We could hear the rumbling of a storm approaching. Looking up at the sky, we saw sand lifting on the horizon from a downdraft and growing in size. We grabbed our cameras and climbed on the roof of the house to see the full force of this sand wall coming straight at us. It was a huge wave, an amazing sight! Seconds before the sand hit us, we jumped off the roof and sought refuge inside the house, closing doors and windows to prevent it from blowing in. A few minutes after the Haboob passed, the storm itself arrived with pounding rain on the tin roof making so much noise we couldn't hear ourselves talk.

Because of the flooded ground, aidworkers had to once again rely on the Twin Otter to move from one location to the next, so we were flying more frequently. As usual, the very short rotations between Goz Beida and Koukou were increased. But to the north it was the never-ending instability of Guéréda that kept us busy. More attacks and more shooting meant more medevac flights. Even with all the horrors I'd witnessed, this day's experience is one I can never forget. And it wasn't from what I saw, but more from what I smelled. One of the wounded we picked up was loaded on the plane, his legs bandaged. Something had made them turn a strange array of colours varying from yellow to brown and everything in between. Thick fluid was leaking from his wounds, and when I saw my colleague's face, I knew I had to help this patient aboard.

I had him sit while I attached the seat belt around his waist. Placing myself behind him once he was seated, I grabbed the seatbelt and, while holding my breath, clipped it together. The smell of his rotting flesh made me gag, and I had to quickly exit the plane to regain my composure. I closed the passenger door and, after a few deep breaths, climbed into the cockpit. When I looked back to see if everyone was comfortable and ready for departure, the patient looked at me, his eyes empty. With a shy smile in the corner of his mouth, he gave me a thumbs up. Not once did I hear him moan or groan. I don't know how he was managing the pain.

Around this time, I found myself struggling with my health again. I was losing weight, but with no other signs of discomfort other than occasional diarrhoea, I chalked it up to the heat and a busy work schedule.

After a night of thunder and lightning, the sun had risen, and we were preparing for yet another flight to the north. Guéréda was our first stop, so I consulted our security officer on the daily situation there. He notified me of more fighting in the area, and I saw two Chadian military helicopters take-off just before our departure. They seemed to be setting course toward our destination. Their pilots were mainly from Russia or South America, so their English was limited and they didn't speak French. Not that it mattered much, since they rarely spoke to us and would never answer our radio calls. This was very frustrating as we never really knew where they were, and their camouflage paint made them difficult to spot from the air.

As we approached Guéréda, I scanned the horizon and checked out the runway while turning on final approach. Everything looked clear and normal. Once we were set to land, we suddenly saw a cloud of dust lift up from the ground and realized that the two helicopters were landing there too. Instead of using the runway, they settled down on a small area used for parking next to the airstrip. The runway was clear, so we landed and taxied to the ramp to park in the only available spot left between the two of them. I kept an eye on the truck full of soldiers around the helicopters while disembarking our passengers and checking in the ones for pick up. We didn't know exactly what was happening, but the potential volatility of the situation called for quick action. The sooner we could get back in the air and out of there, the better.

The ground was very soft due to the heavy rain the previous night. It was noticeable simply by looking at the small wheels of the heavy helicopter sunk into the mud of the parking area. As soon as everyone was on-board, I started the engines and cautiously taxied onto the runway. I didn't want to slip out of control in the mud and risk a collision with one of the choppers. The runway was in good condition as it was maintained for us. Before reaching the end of the runway I had to make a 180-degree turn to position myself for take-off. As I slowly reduced power while turning the tiller to make my turn, the plane suddenly stopped moving.

I applied more power, but nothing happened. I was at a stand-still. I brought the power back to idle, slid open my side window and looked outside toward the back to see what was wrong. While the ground looked dry on the surface, the sides of the centre runway were soft. Under the dry appearance of the ground, the sand was still wet, and we had sunk right into it even with huge tires. It was classic Murphy's Law in action—this had to happen now, today, with all these soldiers around us gearing up for another fight. I had no other choice but to shut down the engines and step out to assess the situation.

First, we needed to lose some weight. I asked the passengers to step down and wait a few metres off the runway while we dug the plane out of the mud. I borrowed a shovel from the ground staff and started digging in front of the wheels trying to clear a path by removing as much soft earth as we could. I climbed into the cockpit of the empty aircraft and started the engines to see if I could get out of the rut. As I slowly brought the power to the maximum, the Twin Otter moved about a metre and stopped. I shut down the engines again and jumped down to look at the wheels. One side was out and now resting on solid ground, but the other had dug deeper into the sand resulting in a sad looking plane leaning to one side.

We went through the same shovel procedure again, removed more dirt, and I restarted the engines to try it again. This time we succeeded. With a sigh of relief, I turned the plane around and lined up on the runway, ready for take-off. I shut down the engines once more to allow the passengers to board, thanked the ground staff for their help and got airborne out of this troubled spot on the double.

Most of the days in the rainy season started with a bright blue sky, though we could feel humidity in the air. We had to make the most of it in the morning because it usually changed very quickly by midday. Cumulonimbus growing very quickly developed into an afternoon of thunderstorms with build-ups reaching maturity in no time. Sometimes it would then dissipate and leave a calm and clear evening. But if the days were hot enough, all this moisture would start moving again, and another set of storms would roll in after sunset.

Late one evening we were preparing for bed when I heard the rumble of an aircraft in the distance. *That's odd*, I thought. *Who would fly around here at this time?* If anyone did, it would be the Chadian military helicopters or occasionally the French, but not an airplane. I heard the sound a few more times before it disappeared. *Maybe they flew over and kept on going*, I thought. *Very strange.*

The next morning on our way out of the compound to prepare the plane for the day, our gatekeeper said there had been an accident the previous night. We passed a string of curious locals walking along the dusty street toward the airport. Arriving on the tarmac, all I could see was a mass of people standing around the bushes a few hundred metres away, so I hurried over there. There were tire marks on the runway, but instead of being the usual short marks where aircraft touch down upon landing, there was a long stretch of marks extending all the way to the end of the runway indicating a plane had applied its brakes the full length of the runway from its touchdown.

The remains of the plane were a few hundred metres beyond the airstrip, past a small wadi. It was a Chadian military Hercules, the one I had seen offloading material for the troops on the tarmac a few days earlier. All that was left was the tail and part of the wings. Everything else was shredded to pieces or burned; a propeller here, landing gear there, pieces of metal that weren't recognizable and charred bodies. Incredibly, the two pilots had made it out alive, but everyone else in the back hadn't. The plane had been loaded with soldiers, munitions, cargo, and women and children who were family members of the soldiers.

While walking through the smoldering rubble that morning, I watched Red Cross staff cover pieces of bodies, an arm here and a foot there. The sight of a burned woman still holding her baby in her arms shocked me to the core. My brain had a hard time registering what I saw. It felt so unreal. I was processing these images as if watching a movie, but I still had a job to do. Without a word, we were airborne half an hour later. Everyone was quiet and lost in our own thoughts for the rest of the day. A few days later, most of what was left at the crash site had disappeared. Only the wings and tail, which were too big to carry away, remained. Passing over the site was a daily reminder of what had happened.

Abéché Airport was not set up with instrument approaches. If it was, it would have allowed us to take-off and land in poor visibility weather and at night. But it was not the case. With zero lighting on and around the runway, attempting a night landing was madness unless you had night-vision capabilities, which I really doubt the Chadian military had on those aircraft. After three attempts at landing, the Hercules landed a fourth time at the very end of the runway with no chance to either brake and stop in time or bring the power back up to get airborne again.

In the midst of these events that would remain with me forever, I also experienced some memorable and beautiful things. We planned to stay in N'Djamena for a few days while we were there having the Twin Otter repaired. Instead of sitting at our country director's house doing nothing, we decided to venture out for something more exciting. We heard about a national park where a herd of nearly one hundred elephants live not far across the border in Cameroon. I have to admit that the pachyderm is my favourite animal, so I was VERY excited.

We arose early for our adventure in Cameroon and borrowed our director's old car that he only used around town. As he started the engine, the 4x4 made a strange noise. He said not to worry because it always did that. Apparently he had been driving it that way for months without any trouble. We shrugged, and Wade, the other pilot, said, "What the heck, let's have some fun."

I pulled out the hand-drawn sketch of the area we received from a couple of South African aviators, and we hit the road. Just outside the city, we had to cross a bridge marking the boundary between Cameroon and Chad. We had brought our passports with us, but we didn't have a visa to get in. Our friends had told us not to worry because we wouldn't be checked anyway. They were right.

As we slowly drove onto the bridge, we saw police officers and a few soldiers, but no one stopped us or asked us anything, so we kept on going. We passed a few roadblocks on our journey of a couple of hours into the countryside, and with friendly smiles and baksheesh (bribes) to smooth our way, we arrived at the small town marked on our map. The man we asked for directions to enter the park asked if we had paid the permit to enter.

"Ah, non," I said in French. "But tell us where we can get one and we will."

As the only one who spoke French, my partners always let me handle the negotiations. It made me laugh to see their confused expressions when the conversation occasionally heated up. In this case we required a permit to enter the park but couldn't get it there. We had to buy one in a village we passed along the way.

"OK," I said. "But then, once we get it where's the entrance to the park?"

"It's right there, five hundred metres up the road. You'll see a green gate on your left," he said.

With thanks for the information, we got back in the car and turned around. We weren't happy at the prospect of losing over two hours just for a piece of paper, and we knew the fee would likely end up in the pockets of an individual officer, so as we neared the park entrance, we slowed down and noticed the small green gate. With nobody in sight, we followed the tracks in the sand, drove around the gate, and we were in. We were surrounded by bushes and tall trees, and as our truck crawled down that dirt strip, we saw huge piles of dung everywhere. We were definitely at the right place. The vehicle was still making a noise, but I put it out of my mind and focused on elephant spotting. After driving about twenty minutes into the bush we encountered a new gate we certainly couldn't get around. As we approached the gate, I noticed someone sleeping under a tree. He awoke as we stopped and walked slowly toward our car.

"Let me handle this," I said.

The tall, thin man approached, and I opened the window and greeted him with a big smile.

"Bonjour! You're the guide, right? They told us you would be here waiting for us. They said you're the best elephant tracker in the region. We're so happy to be here to have a chance to see them. Just tell me how much we need to pay you and let's go!"

After the initial surprise, he saw his opportunity to make a little money. I knew he had nothing to do with the park, but I knew how everything worked on this continent to benefit all parties. He would show us the herd, make some easy cash, and everyone would be happy at the end of the day. No harm done. He thought for an instant about how much money to request. Seeing that he wasn't sure I simply offered him the equivalent of ten dollars per person. With a big smile, he agreed. *Well, that was easy wasn't it? God, I love Africa!* I thought, laughing to myself. He returned to the tree and picked up his gear, a jacket and a knife that he slid under his shirt in the back of his pants. I offered him a seat in the front and jumped in the back with the other pilots while our director drove.

About half an hour later he told us to stop. Stepping out of the vehicle, he told us to wait. A few seconds later, he disappeared behind the thick bushes. Many minutes passed, and we started to wonder if he had run off with the money and left us there. We killed time by taking pictures and climbing on a large branch that crossed the road above the vehicle. Fifteen minutes later, he finally reappeared. He climbed in the vehicle and simply said, "They're over there!" and pointed in front of us. "Keep driving." We drove for another half hour when he said, "Stop! OK, leave the car here and start walking."

Now we were really wondering if he was just taking us for a joy ride. I mean, we knew he was no park guide—God knows who he was! It was midday and beginning to get hot. We had brought a bottle of water each, but it wasn't enough for a long hike. We walked around bushes and up and down dry riverbeds for about an hour, getting all sweaty and dusty in the process. Suddenly, he said, "Shhh, be very quiet now. They're right there." He pointed a few metres in front of us. At first, we couldn't see anything. But then there was a subtle movement about fifty metres away, and I finally saw the grey skin of a gentle giant.

Gentle, but still wild. I knew that if disturbed they could charge within a blink of an eye. We stuck close together and followed our new friend. Not that he could have done much if anything went wrong. His little knife couldn't save us, but he seemed to know what he was doing so we followed. He walked us around the herd at a safe distance, and when we emerged from the heavy bushes we were beside a river. We could now see the adult females with their young drinking water and a few restless teenagers horsing around. Our guide explained that the lone elephant we had seen earlier was the sentinel, the lookout for the rest of the herd.

Part of the herd started walking into the river, wanting to cross to the other side when suddenly I heard a noise. There were some fishermen on the beach across the river who didn't want the elephants to trample their fishing hole, so they were making a racket to scare them away. Part of the herd was already close to the other side, and the sound of banging tin cups only chased half of them away, which split the group in two. One had crossed the river and the other had returned to the opposite side. They were annoyed, and I saw the sentinel trying to lead them up-river to another crossing spot. They all started walking toward us, and if we hadn't moved right away, we would have been caught in their path with no place to run or hide.

We had to quickly walk farther up the river, faster than they were moving, to remain at a safe distance and get around the herd. Eventually they were out of sight, but we could hear them! They may have been calling to their friends on the other side. Once our guide decided we were at a safe distance, we finally stopped to catch our breath, and we broke into laughter. We were all afraid of what could have happened but overjoyed with what we had just experienced. It was a thrill to be able to get so close to a large herd of elephants and, for an instant, feel like part of their family.

It's very sad to think that poachers hunt elephants down just for ivory in many parts of Africa. Hundreds of them die every day, and the revenue generated from selling their tusks is used to fuel most of the wars on the continent. Multiple weapons, like the AK-47, can be purchased with just one tusk. Tusks can be sold on the Chinese market where the value of ivory is skyrocketing. Elephants are so much more like us than most people may think. Yes, they have an incredible memory, but they also feel and think in ways similar to us. When an elephant dies, for example, the family gathers around seemingly feeling the loss and grieving much like we do. I truly hope that with several organizations trying to help and save them, one day we'll actually manage to stop the killing.

We left these beautiful creatures behind and walked an hour back to our vehicle. From there it took slightly longer than that to drive to the gate where we deposited our friend under his tree again. Back on the main road we headed toward Chad, listening to music and talking about the amazing experience we'd just had.

The noise in our vehicle began to get louder than our music. This wasn't a good sign. Finally, the engine seized-up and stopped, and white fumes streamed from under the hood. It didn't take a genius to figure out what was wrong; there was a hole in the radiator and no more coolant.

Now what? There aren't a lot of repair shops in the African bush. Nobody seemed to know how to fix it, but I remembered an old trick I had learned as a kid when the same thing happened to my mother. Pepper! We only had to make it a few more kilometres down the road to the next village to find a shop with pepper and water. We needed to let the engine cool off, pour the rest of the water we had into the radiator and hope it would last to the village. Once there we would let it cool down again while securing what we needed. Should it hold temporarily, we could make it back into Chad and N'Djamena.

That was the plan. However, three white people sitting on the ground along the road was an unusual sight. The locals passing by kept staring at us, laughing and wondering what we were doing. Some offered to help if they could, but we said we'd be fine. Once the truck cooled we were finally able to get to the next village and secure the pepper and water. Once the radiator had cooled once more, we poured everything in and crossed our fingers. It worked! We were back on the road—at least for now.

The engine started to act up again as we approached Chad, and it kept quitting when we had to slow down in traffic. Because we had to restart the engine again and again to keep moving forward, the battery died a few hundred metres from crossing the bridge and the boundary again. Since our director didn't want to leave the vehicle, we decided to push it. I was the smallest person, so I got behind the wheel while the other three got out and pushed.

All the while, I kept thinking, *Great way to maintain a low profile and be discreet while crossing the border without a visa for Cameroon!*

With everyone looking at us now, we just kept smiling like idiots and crossed the bridge. Look at that! Nobody stopped us or asked anything. They probably thought we were not in the mood to speak given the mechanical problems. Once we were back on Chadian soil, we abandoned the car on the side of the road, not even bothering to lock it. Who would want that piece of shit? We started walking with the hope of flagging down a cab if we saw one.

After thirty minutes, there was still none in sight. It wasn't our lucky day! Hot, sweaty, thirsty, tired, and dirty we stopped at a local bar to grab a drink. We were quite dehydrated. The guy behind the counter heard us talking about the lack of cabs, so he grabbed his phone and called someone. A few minutes later, a taxi driver friend of his pulled up and waited until we finished our drink before offering us a ride back to the city. We couldn't thank them enough!

Back at the house, we needed a good shower before heading to a restaurant. We were very hungry by that point. Of course, over dinner we recounted the adventure of the day. It was amazingly fun but also lucky that, in the end, we had returned safe and sound.

The next day, I went to the hangar and checked with our mechanic on how things were going. He had been doing an amazing job fixing snags, but we had a couple of issues that were becoming quite bad and needed serious repair. Unfortunately, he didn't have the tools for the job there, so we had to consider other options. For now, it was time to fly back to the base in Abéché and resume our daily flights. Meanwhile, our engineer and director discussed what should be done next with headquarters and quickly decided we would fly to Entebbe, Uganda, where the maintenance base for the whole continent was located because they would have the tools and spare parts needed to fix our Twin Otter.

To begin organizing that flight, we needed to decide what route to take. In the past, they had flown first to N'Djamena, then south to Bangui in Central African Republic, across the Democratic Republic of Congo from west to east with one stop in between to refuel, and finally arrived in Uganda. The problem with that plan was the shortage of Jet-A fuel in Bangui—we wouldn't have been able to refuel, so that was a no go.

The only other option I could think of was to fly east from Abéché into Sudan and then south to Uganda. Although it was a shorter route, some didn't like the idea of going into Sudan because of the instability. Complicating matters, the plane was American registered, which was not a good thing in Sudan. There wasn't much choice if we wanted to get the plane fixed quickly and avoid further disruption to our UNHCR contract. I didn't want to impose my idea on the crew, so I discussed it first with my co-pilot and engineer. They agreed and so did home office, so I chose the route with the best refuelling stop.

A rebel group gathering outside of the French military base in Abéché after they took over the town, 2006

On the take-off roll during the rainy season in Goz Beida, Chad

Flying over the crashed Hercules on the morning following the accident. The remaining bodies are covered with blankets, and military personnel are securing the site

Playing with the kids in a remote village while waiting for our VIP passengers to return from their visit at a refugee camp

Flying over one of the biggest refugee camps in eastern Chad

CHAPTER 17

DETAINED

Our director's responsibility was to prepare the permits that allowed us to fly over Darfur into Sudan, the approval to enter Uganda and the landing permits. We also needed enough cash to pay for the fuel, the taxes and our week in Uganda where we had planned to purchase a few items for the house. It was a good occasion to stock up with everything we couldn't find in Chad.

The trip had to be carefully planned, too, because we had also booked a VIP flight for a Swiss delegation, including the president, who was coming to Chad to visit the refugee camps. Our maintenance crew in Entebbe would have five days to work on the plane and get it back in shape to return to Chad in time for that special flight. Complicating matters, our director had a vacation planned, so he wanted to get us everything we needed for the ferry flight before he left. Once he had everything organized, he flew to Abéché and stayed at the compound with us for a few days. He gave me a stash of money to cover the trip and a folder with the necessary documents.

"Good luck in Uganda!" he said as he left for his vacation outside Africa.

It was Tuesday, and we planned to leave early Friday morning for the ferry flight. By Thursday night, we had our plane loaded with spare parts, tires, tools and whatnot. The cargo compartment and the cabin were full with just the front row seat available for our engineer. The next morning would see an early departure with the first two-hour leg taking us across the border to Darfur and stopping in Nyala for fuel and customs. From there, I had planned to continue southbound for about four hours to Rumbek in southern Sudan for another refuelling stop. Then there was one more four-hour flight before crossing into Uganda and arriving at our final destination in Entebbe. In total we would fly close to ten hours and arrive in Entebbe just after dark.

Friday morning, I double-checked that both our satphones as well as our GPS were fully charged, and I grabbed my little bag with spare clothes for the week. I also made sure I had my papers and money and that I hadn't forgotten anything. The three of us were happy and excited to do something different. And we were already looking forward to a good meal of fresh fish and fruit in Uganda, as well as a good bed. Our beds at the house were only a piece of foam, so we sank into the deep holes that formed over time.

We were all curious about what we would see flying over Darfur. So much terror was forcing people to flee across the border into Chad to seek refuge. Following our GPS across the border, we saw burned huts and scarred villages, but Sudan was mostly similar to the desert and dry bush we had become accustomed to. Approaching Nyala, we switched frequencies and made first contact with the tower. After acknowledging who we were and where we were from, the controller asked for our authorization number.

"Stand-by," I said

My co-pilot retrieved the telexed paper containing several coded numbers, and since neither of us had done this before, we were not sure which number they wanted. We radioed the one that appeared to be what they sought, but he didn't sound convinced.

"How about letting us land and you can look at the papers once we're on the ground?" I asked.

"Clear to land," he said, sounding happy enough with the situation.

A few minutes later, we were on final approach for the first landing of the day in Nyala, Sudan. As soon as we exited the runway and pulled onto the parking area, I could sense that something was wrong. Following a marshaled indicator, I stopped and shut down the engine. As soon as the propellers wound down, we found ourselves surrounded by soldiers aiming their rifles at us. A tall man walked to my door. I didn't want to show signs of fear or stress, so I opened my door and greeted him with a smile. Returning it in kind, he asked me to show him our landing permit, which I did, keeping my eyes trained on what was going on around us. Someone had already popped open our back door and was glancing inside to see what we were carrying. As he looked around, I quickly explained that these items were parts for our plane that we were ferrying to Uganda for repairs at our maintenance base.

The tall man, who was, in fact, the airport manager, looked at the papers I had handed him. Losing his smile, he now looked at me sternly and said, "This is not an approved landing permit. It's only a request for one." *Shit, shit, shit!* I thought. My teammates and I looked at each other and knew we were in trouble. He asked me to follow him, and I was escorted to the control tower. I did so without question, telling the crew to watch over the plane and stay put. As we walked across the tarmac, the airport manager played nice and pretended it was no big deal.

"I'll call the appropriate authorities and we'll clear you quickly, you'll see!" he said while staring at me with a creepy fake smile.

I followed him to the control room on top of the tower—at least I had a nice view to keep an eye on the Twin Otter and my crew. They had me sit outside their office where the little game continued.

"Here, try our tea, it's the best. And have some of our local cookies with it. You must accept. It's our culture!"

I played along but wasn't in the mood for tea and biscuits. I wanted to fix this mess and get out of there! He casually grabbed the phone and made a few calls. I had no idea to whom, or what he was saying because he spoke in Arabic, but I wasn't going to trust that the problem would soon be resolved. He then asked me to be patient and sit tight as he waited for someone to return his call.

An hour went by, then two and three. Nothing happened. Of course, nothing would happen because it was Friday, the holy day in Muslim countries. Probably nothing would occur anywhere there until at least Monday. Jake, my co-pilot, had had enough of waiting for my return. He was beginning to worry about my whereabouts, so he came looking for me. They offered him tea and cookies too.

"Yeah, I know!" I said, when he looked puzzled at the scene.

After talking for another hour, they finally agreed to let me return to the aircraft, and we joined our engineer. He was pacing around the Twin Otter while under the watch of an armed guard. I sat in the cockpit, grabbed the satellite phone in the side pocket of my door and called our chief pilot in Entebbe. He had no idea that we were stuck there and not on our way south.

He advised me to hang in there while he called headquarters in the States to find a solution to this situation. We knew the rest of the day would be a long waiting game. We had no food and were tapping into our water supply packed on-board for the trip. I managed to convince the airport manager to let me at least refuel the airplane. It's not that I was going to fly away that day, but at least it would be filled and ready for whenever we were released. When I handed over a pile of twenty-dollar bills for the fuel, the agent took his time and checked every note. He pulled out three quarters of them and handed them to me saying, "Those are no good, too old, give me new bills!"

In many African countries they don't accept bills if they're older than a certain year. It varies from country to country, so it was always best to bring the newest bills you could find. My country director hadn't thought of that, and he gave us whatever he had in his safe. Not only were we stuck in Sudan for God knows how long, but most of the money I had to cover the cost of our trip was unusable. Great! Just awesome! This was getting better by the minute. Luckily for him he wasn't there with us or I would have ripped his head off.

We waited under a burning sun on the tarmac for a phone call with positive news. We were hot, hungry and losing hope. Meanwhile, they asked us to submit our passports for processing. That made me nervous, and I refused to let the documents out of my sight. I followed them to the office and insisted on waiting there until they had processed and returned them to us. They might have been able to detain us for now, but that didn't mean I would let them do whatever they wanted. Later, our chief pilot confirmed they had been in contact with the Sudanese authorities in Khartoum and were working toward a solution.

The Swiss government had also been contacted to pressure the Sudanese to release us quickly. It was because I am Swiss, but also because we were due to fly the Swiss president in for a visit to Chad in a few days. From what I was told, the Sudanese didn't give a shit and turned the Swiss down.

With the sun going down, I started to wonder what they would do with us. We wouldn't be able to keep an eye on our plane and its cargo, which worried me, but there was nothing we could do. We grabbed our personal travel pack, and the engineer and I each took a satphone. I split the money reserve amongst the crew to hide safely in various places. Finally, before walking away from the Twin Otter, I locked the doors.

We were taken out of the airport into the parking area where a car was waiting for us. The airport manager wished us a good night and said he would see us in the morning. Two military trucks escorted us off the main road leading to the city centre and pulled into an isolated compound about half an hour later. Our guard exchanged a few words in Arabic with the person behind a desk in the building, and he left us there.

The place looked like some sort of hotel or guesthouse, but it had a strange feeling. There was a large, long hallway with rooms spread on both sides and a huge dining table in the middle that was already set for the three of us. The whole place was so quiet we could hear flies buzzing. We were alone in this complex, and if it hadn't been for the guards keeping watch outside, I could have forgotten that we were under arrest. We were so hungry that whatever they served us was heaven sent. We kept talking about our situation, thinking over what went wrong, what we could have done differently to avoid this, what we should do now and what we could expect to happen next. It was out of our hands, so all we could do was remain calm, sit tight and hope for the best. We had people working for us and needed to trust that they would do everything in their power to get us freed.

We were exhausted, so we went to bed soon after dinner, but I couldn't shut down my brain as I laid in bed. Our predicament spun around my head like a desert wind. The relentless sound of mosquitoes was aggravating as there was no mosquito net. There was no air conditioning, so the room never cooled down from the heat of the day. When I got up next morning and walked into the hallway, the crew didn't need to exchange words. None of us had slept. Breakfast was served, and we ate all we could because we didn't know when our next meal would be. After breakfast, a car waited outside to escort us back to the airport.

Here we go again! We resumed our positions on the tarmac next to the Twin Otter and walked to the tower office every so often for updates. It was another exhausting and frustratingly long day. The airport authorities must have received information that told them we wouldn't be released any time soon because they said we had to find our own place to stay while we were detained. I figured they didn't want to keep paying for our food and lodging.

A Twin Otter I had seen in Abéché a few months earlier was also parked at the airport. It was a Swiss company flying under the Red Cross flag, so I thought they might be willing to give us a hand. The mechanic was working on his plane, so I walked up and introduced myself. After explaining our situation, I asked if they could give us one room for the night; all three of us could crash together. We had money for food so all we really needed was a roof over our heads. He looked at me blankly and said, "Sorry, there's nothing I can do for you."

I was stunned. Really? He wasn't willing to help fellow aviators who happened to be stranded? *Unbelievable*, I thought. So much for the humanitarian spirit! I walked away without wasting anymore thoughts. I called our chief pilot on the satphone for updates and to ask him to contact UNHCR in Nyala to request a room for the night.

An Ilyushin 76 was parked across the tarmac, and its crew was sitting on lawn chairs under the wings for shade. They were joyfully sipping drinks and waving vodka bottles over their heads, inviting us to join them. Damn Russians! I had to laugh though, as they had just confirmed the stereotype of the drunken Russian pilots. I would have loved to join them, however, just for a chance to tour their crazy looking aircraft. I reminded myself that we were under constant watch, and it wasn't wise to step out of sight from the guards.

"Hey! Sky Hunter, come have a drink with us!" one of the Russians yelled as he waved a bottle of vodka.

I slowly walked toward them, and we managed to have a friendly discussion while staying in plain sight next to their aircraft. Their English was limited, but I had to ask them why they had just called me Sky Hunter. He simply said that I had to be mad and hunting for the sky because there were no other good reasons to be in this godforsaken place.

There were a few other aircraft bearing the UN logo. On the other side of the airport, the military had a few jet fighters, possibly A-5 Fantans, and they were also busy loading Mi-24 attack helicopters with heavy ammunition. It appeared they were getting ready for a battle somewhere. In the far corner, a white Antonov 26, registered ST-ZZZ, stood alone. The sight of it gave me chills as for the past few months I'd been hearing stories about it. According to some reports there were actually three aircraft with that same registration—and they weren't used for humanitarian purposes. On numerous occasions we'd been told to keep our eyes open when flying along the border because locals reported that the "white" airplanes were bombing villages.

So here we were in the middle of this surreal afternoon under the burning sun when we should have been in Uganda enjoying a "Nile Special" while sitting around the pool. A UNHCR representative finally arrived to pick us up at sundown. The airport authorities let us go with him but not before they demanded to know exactly where we would be staying, warning us not to go anywhere else. *Where would we go, really!?*

We were a bit more relaxed now that we were not under constant watch by the Sudanese military. On the way to the compound, we stopped in town to exchange some local money and replenish our food and water. We were offered a room to stay overnight but nothing more. The UNHCR employee lived alone in a big house because everyone else had been evacuated a few weeks earlier. He showed us our room and gave us a little speech about his house rules. He also made sure we understood that he was doing this because he had to, not because he wanted to. He then walked out, leaving us to our own devices regarding anything else we might need. That was fine by us. We were just happy to be out of the torturing heat on the tarmac. After cooking ourselves dinner, we retreated to our beds for the night.

The next morning, I told the crew to use the spare satphone to call their families. I knew they wanted to check-in with them and let them know they were fine. I also hoped it would help them relax a bit. I had no family to speak of and wasn't prepared to call any friends and cause panic over this ordeal, so I preferred to give my airtime to our engineer who had a wife and kids at home. Jake was sitting outside enjoying a drink, and Mat was talking to his wife on the back patio when our boss called. The president of our company got on the line with the latest news, but mainly to say he knew and understood how we felt. He was well aware of the dangers of having a US-registered plane in Sudan—one of the three countries in the world least friendly to the west at that point.

He told me he had a similar episode and understood the stress of our situation. He asked how everyone was doing and assured me that everything was being done to secure our release. However, he had no way of knowing how long it would take. I said that, while Jake and I were fine, I wondered if there was any way he could negotiate Mat's release as soon as possible because I was afraid he was going to lose it. He was—understandably—freaking out because he had a family back home. Of course, release was wishful thinking, and all I could do to keep them calm was hide my own fear, keep smiling and remain positive. We spent the whole day sitting around with nothing to do again, not even a book to read. Sometimes we sat together and talked. At other times we needed to retreat alone with our thoughts, lying on the concrete floor outside or sitting on a wooden chair in the back of the house.

The hours passed slowly, and after one more sleepless night, day four began the same way the previous ones had. It was Monday so I was hoping something would happen. All we got that day was, "Hang tight. We're on it!" It was another day of staring at the walls, tired, bored and depressed.

The sound of our phone ringing woke us on Tuesday. It was our chief pilot calling from Entebbe to tell us there was a good chance we would be released that day and to stand by for confirmation. It wasn't a done deal, but it motivated us to make a plan. First, we needed a cab to get back to the airport. It didn't matter if we had to wait there all day again and return at night if the flight failed to materialize. We just wanted to be there, ready to fly in case it came through.

We packed our bags, squished into the back seat of a tiny taxi and headed for the airport. I checked in with the airport authorities and requested permission to access our aircraft, notifying them of our release. Acknowledging that they were also standing by for final confirmation, we were allowed to walk out of the building onto the tarmac but not yet access the parking to check on the plane. I was concerned that someone might have tried to gain access or vandalize it, but from a distance it looked as we had left it a few days earlier.

The phone kept ringing in the office, but nobody said the words we needed to hear. Meanwhile, I devised a schedule for the long flight to Entebbe. The latest we could leave was two o'clock in the afternoon. That would give us time to fly to Rumbek for a refuelling stop and resume flying again before nightfall, as the runway had no lighting. At lunchtime our chief pilot called to say our release was imminent, though we had to wait just a little longer. This waiting game was getting on our nerves, but I didn't want to lose hope. We sat down, ate the sandwiches prepared for the trip and kept staring at the horizon in the direction we hoped to go.

At 1:30, we figured we'd have to stay at least one more night. Was this ever going to end? How long were they going to keep us here? Weeks? Months? Pessimism began to cloud my brain, and I hated it. At 1:50, our chief called and said, "It's done. You're released and free to go!"

That was awesome news, but it wasn't time to celebrate. If we wanted to leave that day, we needed to hear it from the authorities who were holding us. I hung up the phone, told the crew the good news and walked to the tower to find the manager. Of course, he hadn't yet received the green light, so I demanded he call immediately. A few minutes later, he confirmed that we were finally released.

He followed me out of the office where we saw Jake and Mat standing outside with our luggage. Three soldiers had refused them access to the aircraft. I asked what was going on and, after talking to his soldiers, the manager turned to me and said they hadn't received any information—and they needed to be paid.

Of course! Now it was bribe time.

I angrily told him they had better settle this now because I needed to be airborne within fifteen minutes, otherwise they would have to pay for another night's room and board. We were officially released, so they had no right to detain us. He knew I was right and realized he had to do something fast. He quickly said something to his assistant, looked at me briefly while nodding, then approached the soldiers. With backs turned to us he discussed the situation with them. Meanwhile, his assistant quietly told us to grab our bags and throw them in the back of his pickup. We quickly jumped in and left. He drove us the few hundred metres across the tarmac to our plane, said "Good luck" and left.

I was stunned, but I didn't want to waste one second. Mat opened the back door, threw our bags in and got on-board. Jake walked around the plane to remove the covers and jumped in fast once he checked the exterior. I was already in the cockpit starting up the engines. Two minutes later, we taxied onto the runway while peering nervously at the two Mi-24 helicopters that also roared to life. Jake quickly called our chief pilot in Uganda to let him know we would be airborne soon. We also needed him to notify Rumbek of our arrival and to have the fuel truck waiting. Meanwhile, I received the "Clear to take-off" from the control tower.

We hastily rolled down the runway. The blades of the two helicopters were turning at full speed now, and their pilots requested take-off approval from Control as well. I had a bad feeling about this, and a chill ran down my spine. As soon as we were airborne, I turned in a direction off of our normal track while climbing. The possibility of getting shot down was definitely in our minds. Maybe it was paranoia due to the lack of sleep over the previous five days, but I wasn't taking any chances. As soon as we were out of sight of the airport, I turned the transponder off so they wouldn't be able to track us on their TCAS. I dove down low, flying just off the ground, and got back on our track for long enough to believe we were out of their reach. When we eventually climbed to cruising altitude and were well on our way, I finally relaxed. We were free again.

The farther south we flew, the greener the landscape appeared. It was July in the middle of the rainy season, which meant unstable weather and thunderstorms. With all the last-minute delay, we had taken off at 2:30 p.m., which meant we would arrive in Rumbek around 6:30. I hoped the fuel company would wait for us, as they normally shut down for the day at six o'clock. It also meant we would have only minutes to spare before getting back into the air, as night would fall before seven. Luckily, we had a stiff tailwind pushing us south that helped us regain some lost time.

When we approached the airstrip for landing, it was 6:20. Perfect! Even better, I could see the fuel truck waiting in the parking lot. Pulling in right next to it, I shut down the engines and opened my door. I was about to present myself but, without giving me the time to say hello, the fuel handler handed me a cell phone and said, "It's for you." It was our chief pilot who, keeping on top of things, was happy to hear we had made it that far. I confirmed we would resume our flight within twenty minutes and gave him an approximate time of arrival in Entebbe. He knew that flying over South Sudan at night was uncommon, so he gave me the final authorization number to enter Ugandan airspace and wished us a good flight. He planned to meet us upon arrival at Entebbe International Airport.

With our aircraft refuelled, we rolled down the runway and were back in the air as the sun dipped below the horizon. At this latitude, it didn't take long before darkness set in. We settled in at cruising altitude for the four-and-a-half-hour flight. Mat was asleep in the back, but Jake and I had no time to relax. Not yet! We found ourselves in the middle of a storm system without knowing exactly where the storms were. One of the reasons for this trip was to fix our radar that had stopped working a few weeks prior, so we spent the next few hours flying blind on a dark night in and out of clouds with only flashes of lightning to light up the sky. Besides a few rare lights from small villages on the ground, it was complete darkness. I was exhausted, and all I could think of was getting to sleep for as long as my body needed. Jake and I constantly monitored our instruments to make sure we were still on course; we didn't have the strength to talk. Besides the humming of the engines, it was dead silent in the cockpit. The turbulence from the storms was getting so strong that Mat woke up. We all just crossed our fingers and hoped we would come out of it in one piece.

As we approached the Ugandan border, I tuned into their frequency and called Entebbe control. After an acknowledgment, I gave them my position, altitude, destination and estimated time of arrival, along with our authorization number.

"Copied OK, call us back sixty miles inbound, maintain nine thousand feet, and welcome to Uganda," the controller said.

Only one more hour and we'd be there. I was so looking forward to landing this bird and calling it a day. I could finally see the lights of Kampala on the left side as we started our descent, and then we caught sight of the coast of Lake Victoria. A warm feeling engulfed me when I finally saw the runway lights of Entebbe Airport straight ahead. It was close to midnight when we touched down.

I followed our parking instructions, shut down the engines and turned toward the crew. They smiled back at me. We had made it! As soon as I opened the door and jumped down from the cockpit, our chief pilot arrived and gave me the biggest hug I had ever received on this job. He was happy, but probably not as happy as we were! It was time to eat and then off to bed. I hadn't slept in days.

CHAPTER 18

TIME TO GO

All this delay didn't change the fact that we had to fly back to Chad on Friday. The Swiss delegation was still due to visit on Saturday, so it was up to maintenance to make up for lost time. They basically had two days to work on the plane instead of the whole week they initially planned. Obviously, there was no way they could get everything done in such a short time, but they would work day and night until our departure to at least fix the major issues.

In the meantime, Jake and I enjoyed relaxing at the hotel pool and visiting the beautiful Entebbe Botanical Gardens. We also had a list of items to purchase for our house in Abéché, so we drove to a mall in Kampala. After having been secluded in the desert for so long, it felt overwhelming to be surrounded by so many people. The traffic and noise of the big city made my head spin.

I went to the hangar on Thursday afternoon to check on the progress of the Twin Otter. The maintenance crew had worked non-stop for the previous couple of days and were making great progress. One of the issues was the steering system. The Twin Otter uses a tiller to turn the front wheel on the ground at slow speed in order to line up on the runway for takeoff. It had become difficult to steer over the previous few months, and Mat hadn't been able to release the tension with his available tools. To make a full turn, I had to pull so hard on the tiller that I ended up getting tendonitis in my left wrist, and it wasn't healing due to the constant force I kept putting on it when working. I really wanted this corrected before we left, as I knew it would probably be a long time before another trip to Uganda could be arranged.

After it was fixed, I had to do a high-speed taxi run to make sure the nose wheel and steering was behaving normally. After approval from the control tower, I taxied onto an unused runway and applied power, bringing the plane almost to the speed of take-off before stopping again. Making slow turns felt promising at first because I had to apply substantially less pressure. But as soon as I picked up speed, the nose gear started shaking violently; simply a no go. They would have to work again all night to correct it by early morning.

While it was another long night for the maintenance crew, I was able to retire early that night. I expected a long day of flying the next day, and I hoped to avoid other problems along the way. Of course, I wasn't going to stop in Nyala again, so I had to find another way to make it home without that fuelling stopover. There weren't many choices, and the fact that we were flying against the wind this time didn't help.

At six o'clock Friday morning, I was back on the runway doing another test. This time it was satisfactory. While the maintenance department signed off on the logbook and paperwork, Mat, Jake and I loaded the plane with our bags and groceries. An hour later we were in the air and settling in for a long flight due north. We would have only one fuel stop instead of two, so our second leg was going to be a long stretch, and I had to keep a close eye on fuel management. There would be little fuel to spare, and I marked a specific decision point where we would either be good to continue or would have to turn back to avoid running out of fuel.

We flew to Wau first, a very pleasant early-morning flight in smooth air and clear sky. I let the guys supervise the refuelling while I walked over to the office to pay the taxes. It was also my last chance to find a bathroom. Guys can always pee in an empty bottle while in flight, but that's not so practical for us ladies! I walked over to a little shack that appeared to be a toilet. It was basically a hut with a hole cut in the floor, a pit a few metres deep and barely enough room to turn around once the door was closed. There was a tiny window high on a back wall of mud and sticks. The odour hit me, stinging my eyes and causing me to gag. It was horrendous, but I had no choice; there weren't any bushes for miles.

I took a deep breath, held it, went in and closed the door. I was glad nobody could see my face right then, cheeks bulging. Before pulling up my pants again, I had to breathe. So, thrusting my face out the small window, I gasped for air and held my breath again. I was just glad I wasn't constipated. I broke free and let out my breath.

Back at the plane, Jake asked me where the bathroom was. I just pointed at and said, "Have fun!"

Forty-five minutes later we were back in the air. To avoid Nyala, I planned to fly straight from Wau to Abéché. This would amount to nearly five hours of flight time, meaning we would land low on fuel with no chance to divert if we couldn't land upon arrival (not that there were many alternative airstrips around anyway).

My flight plan took us right over Goz Beida, one of our daily destinations. At that point, we would either have enough fuel to continue on to Abéché or, if it looked like we might run too low to cover the last hour of flight, we could land there and use our emergency fuel that was stashed in barrels at the UNHCR compound. However, because the weather was favourable that day, we managed to cover the trip without that unscheduled extra stop and arrived in Abéché by the end of the afternoon as planned.

Home sweet home! Work was not over yet though. We still had to offload the plane and give it a good clean in preparation for the Swiss delegation. The next morning, the three of us were still tired from the long, stressful week we had endured, but we arose early and donned clean white shirts to look our best for the VIPs.

The end of the rainy season saw me enjoying a more relaxed time. Besides the odd medical evacuation, we were just flying our normal routes, and nothing out of the ordinary was happening. The only concern I had was my health. It had been a year since I'd had my gall bladder removed. Though I knew it would change how my body reacted to certain foods, digesting red meat or spicy food became particularly difficult. I adjusted my eating habits but was still struggling to keep my weight up. I was soon due for my next R&R and, as I was not going back to Canada, I planned to spend ten days in Europe between Switzerland and France. I made an appointment with my aviation doctor for the annual medical check for my European pilot license and would take that chance to discuss my constant weight loss.

Deep down I knew it would soon be time to leave Chad and do something else. As much as I loved the job it was just not healthy to keep at it much longer. I remembered the Swiss company who also owned Twin Otters working in different parts of Africa, so I contacted them and set up an interview for the same week I was in Switzerland.

The first stop, of course, was my doctor. After pronouncing me "fit" for the aviation medical test, he prescribed other tests to figure out what was going on. It made me nervous because I was afraid to hear something unexpected again; the prospect of needing further surgery was not enticing. The results from the tests indicated I had contracted two different parasites (which explained the weight loss and gall-stones), but they were treatable with antibiotics. The bad news was that the parasites had been in me for so long, my liver might have been affected. He sent me for an ultrasound.

While I awaited the results, I drove to the other side of the country and went for the job interview. They are a much larger organization and employ over one hundred pilots. They also operated under tighter European regulations. Despite their size, their working environment looked more like that of a bush company. Every pilot working for them maintained high standards, taking multiple courses and undergoing various checks each year. I also liked their stability, conditions under which I had never worked before, and their rotational shifts of five weeks at work followed by five weeks off.

One of the conditions of employment was to move to Europe, which meant leaving Canada for good. Despite finding this a little strange (they had employees in Canada), I didn't object because I could have easily moved if necessary. By the end of the day they had already taken my picture for a crew badge and my size for the uniform, so I thought this looked quite promising. Before I left, they assured me I would hear from them with a decision soon. With that in mind, I drove the four hours back to see my doctor for the test results.

He said I was very fortunate, as it appeared my liver was free of damage. All I had to do was follow the two-week antibiotic treatment and I would be back in shape in no time.

The Swiss aviation company called me the next morning and offered a position that began right away. I was very pleased about it, not because I was leaving Chad and the job I had loved these past two years, but because it meant that the experience I had accumulated there was of great interest to potential employers. My aviation career was taking off!

Everything moved quickly when I returned to Abéché. I gave my two-weeks notice to terminate my contract, and between flying every day, packing my stuff and saying goodbyes, I didn't have much time to think about it. When I finally realized this was my last goodbye to Chad, I was sitting on-board the Air France flight that took me back to Europe again.

I had held off the antibiotic treatment temporarily because they weren't compatible with driving, not to mention flying. But I had to take the next two weeks to complete the cycle and restore my health. Meanwhile, I started looking for a place to stay and already knew approximately where I would live. Daniel and I had kept in touch, and our relationship was still alive while he was in France. He was in a similar situation as I was, and I thought I would give it a chance to see where this relationship might lead. And honestly, there were worse places to live than southeast France, so what the heck? If I had to relocate to Europe it might as well be on the beautiful Côte d'Azur!

Organizing everything I had to do before starting my new job didn't afford enough time to drive south and visit places to rent, but I scoured the internet looking for a studio or small condo and made a few phone calls. In the meantime, I was sent for Crew

Resource Management (CRM), Emergency and Safety Equipment Training (ESET), Dangerous Goods (DG) and various other courses. A fun part was the day at the pool where I had to don a life vest, swim to a raft and try to board without flipping it. I was small and light, so it wasn't too difficult, but watching the heavier guys try it was hilarious. I also spent a day playing with fire and using various types of extinguishers. What wasn't as much fun was the re-enactment of escaping from a plane filled with smoke. A forty-foot long container had been set up as an airliner cabin with rows of passenger seats. They sent us in normally in teams of two. However, because there was an odd number of students someone had to go in alone. Guess who that was. Thanks, guys; the joy of being the only woman in the group—it never failed!

Without knowing the exact set-up, I had to enter from one end holding a bottle of water and breathing through a gas mask. The goal was to get to the other end of the cabin, find the fire, extinguish it, turn around, find the body of an unconscious passenger and drag the dummy back out with me through the same door I entered. Most of the team had already done the exercise, and one of them had frantically pounded on the door to exit as soon as he got in. When my turn came, I heard comments that I'd never make it, especially while going in alone. I smiled and thought, *You don't know me!*

I stepped into the container, and the door slammed behind me. I found myself in total darkness, surrounded by the thick smoke. I didn't want to go into panic mode, so I concentrated on my breathing. Step by step, I advanced into the cabin, feeling my way to get an idea of how the seats were arranged. When I finally reached the other end, I couldn't see the fire, though I felt the heat of the barrel where it was supposed to be. At the same time a side door popped open and someone threw a burning newspaper in, the door closing again.

"Ha, that was funny. Thanks, guys! Got my fire now!" I said pouring my bottle of water to extinguish it and turning around for mission two. Now I had to find the body. Of course, I wasn't alone in that space. For security reasons, a fireman wearing an infrared camera was following my progress. I couldn't see him but, at some point, I heard him breathe down my neck. It gave me the creeps! Checking the seats one by one, I finally found the dummy and pulled it toward me. God, that thing was heavy! I scrambled the last few metres back to the starting point while dragging the dummy behind me. As I tried to exit, the door didn't open.

"Hey! I'm done! Open the door!" I yelled.

The door slowly opened eventually, and I surmised they just wanted to play around with me a little longer. The entire drill had taken only a few minutes, though it felt more like an hour. But I had made it and walked out with a big smile on my face.

Next, I had to get on a plane for a quick training flight before flying a check ride to revalidate my European license for a Twin Otter rating. The plan was to do it within the following few days, but as I was still on antibiotics, I couldn't. I needed another week before my head was clear enough for the cockpit. The treatment was so strong that just walking along a street was hard enough; at times I suddenly felt like the ground was giving away below me.

A week later I was in the cockpit, finished my training and had passed my flight test. Once that training phase was over, I had just enough time to settle down in my new place before being sent on my first rotation. I rented a car and drove eight hours south to Provence, France, where I was scheduled to meet with the owner of a small studio.

As soon as I reached the coast, the sight of the Mediterranean made me feel like I was on vacation and brought back memories of my childhood. The sound, the smell, the warmth, I loved it. This was my new home!

That evening I set my luggage down in the small fourteen-square-metre furnished studio. It was just big enough for a folding bed, a cupboard, a kitchenette with bar and a bathroom separated by a curtain from the rest of the room. I spent the next few days getting settled and walking along the beach just across the street from my building. Perfect. I was happy.

A week later I returned my rental car to the Nice Airport and flew out to my first posting.

CHAPTER 19

SAHARA

After a layover in Paris, I boarded the plane that brought me directly to my job site in Hassi Messaoud, Algeria, in the middle of the Sahara Desert. I'd been in the desert before while flying north of Abéché in Chad, but it was nothing like this. I was truly in the middle of it. All I could see in any direction was sand dunes for miles on end. The sky in Hassi was darkened by the constant burning of oil from production plants that were surrounding the town. The air was dry, and the temperature pleasant during the day, but as soon as the sun went down, the mercury dropped quickly, sometimes below freezing. It was winter.

Every expatriate working for the oil and gas industry shared the daily life of a base camp. Some camps were larger than others and had amenities like a gym or pool, while others were very basic. I would alternate between them. A restaurant served breakfast, lunch and dinner at fixed hours, and outside of that, unless you had your own food reserve in your container room, you had to wait until the next mealtime. The majority of the crews stayed in the main camp in Hassi, but a few aircraft were based on rig sites.

Those pilots lived in remote camps, staying mostly in container rooms when not flying. With luck you'd have a TV and even internet, but that wasn't always the case, so I always brought a few books to keep busy with while waiting out those long hours between flights. And this is also variable; on projects with certain clients, I would fly a lot, whereas with others I would spend most of my time on stand-by.

At first, I wasn't assigned a specific client but remained based in Hassi Messaoud and flew a dedicated charter aircraft. I worked with a training captain who showed me the ropes and the multi-crew standard procedures of the company. I was also flying with him to the various sites I might be asked to fly once I was signed-off. Flying for the oil and gas industry required strict training and experience. I also soon realized that young aviators working as co-pilots with the company would likely be stuck in the co-pilot seat for years, as it was nearly impossible to acquire sufficient time in the left seat for an upgrade.

Luckily, my previous experience on the Twin Otter provided plenty of hours, and having already flown in the African desert I was the perfect candidate for the company. I accomplished the required training hours in just over a week and soon received my first assignment to an outside base, temporarily covering for another pilot until the end of my five-week rotation. I flew a half-hour flight three days a week from the main hub in Hassi, so I finished my day's work before lunch.

I spent the rest of my days in a room without a TV or a heater and with nothing much to do. My co-captain had a room across the hall from mine, and we either read or conversed from a distance so we could stay under the blankets for warmth. I quickly became bored and started counting the days 'til I'd return home. It sure was a long way from all the fun and excitement of Chad, and I was already missing it.

Back in France I took the time to get to know my new neighbourhood and prepared everything I needed to live there. I bought a small car and enjoyed relaxing in Provence. I wasn't spending much time inside my small, uncomfortable place that was mainly appropriate for eating and sleeping. I knew it was temporary, a place to start. But now that I was on site, I could try to find something better and more permanent. I could only stay there until the end of April anyway because most condo owners along the coast rented by the month during the winter, but by the week during tourist season. They made a fortune.

My five weeks off came and went so quickly that I was on my way back to the same base in the "sand pit" in no time. As it was nearing the end of the project it would probably be my last rotation there. I was flying more this time and, as a result of the project ending, there were a few VIP flights to various sites. I learned a lot on these special flights in the past, and here was no exception. However, I hated the disorganization and lack of ability to keep on schedule. Not that I wasn't flexible. But a flight ending up with an overnight at a different base without prior notification wasn't something we appreciated. That particular week we flew around the region and slept in different beds every night. We returned to our base only on the third day, finally able to obtain a change of clothes before heading back out again. From then on, I learned to keep a spare shirt and travel essentials in my flight bag at all times.

I also learned more about the dynamics between the people with whom I worked, both clients and co-workers, on that second rotation. Their mindsets were so different from what I had previously experienced. Until now I'd been flying with the purpose of helping people, and it didn't matter if my salary was low. Everyone in this company was mainly in it for the money and the time off between rotations. I soon realized that when the motivation was money, no one cared about anything else.

I liked the job. Well…I liked that I was working as a pilot and flying a Twin Otter, the plane I love so much. For the first time in my life I was making a good salary that allowed me to finally save for my future. But such a big company that included over one hundred pilots hailing from so many different cultures created an unhealthy environment. The French didn't like the Italians because the Italians hated the French. The Germans were in the middle, and everyone else was trying to fit in somewhere. I didn't approve of all the backstabbing between fellow aviators and being forced to choose a side. Sadly, like everyone else I was now just in it for the money.

I focused on doing my job as best as I could and never expected anything more than salary in return. I got used to rotational work—five weeks away from home and working hard, followed by five weeks enjoying my quiet life in France—but I wished I was enjoying it more. With extra money in my hands and lots of free time, I could have travelled or taken part in all sorts of activities. But my goal was to save because I had started a new life all over again with empty pockets after arriving in Europe on my own. In addition, I was already travelling every five weeks and pretty much living out of a suitcase, so I just wanted to stay put and relax during my time off.

What I found really difficult was the pace of life that came with the job. They were go, go, go! days on duty, then suddenly nothing. My first week home I was usually so tired from my rotation that I just caught up on sleep and rested. But then an adrenaline crash would result in me starting to feel depressed and bored. At work I was surrounded with people, co-workers and clients. Back home I was alone. My so-called relationship with Daniel hadn't lasted. I had eventually figured out that it was all just a game for him, and we weren't at all on the same page regarding the future.

I really enjoyed Provence though, and on sunny days I would head to the beach for a few hours. I had found a little apartment that was part of a villa in a village about twenty minutes from the coast. The countryside was peaceful and quiet. Walking along the olive groves, the smell of mimosa in the spring, rosemary and thyme in the summer was so relaxing. The owners were very nice and looked out for me. The months passed very fast; it seemed that time sped up when going back and forth every few weeks.

Back at work, I was glad to see the end of the sandstorm season. Even though I sort of enjoyed the challenges that came with it, the feeling of sand invading everything wasn't fun. With summer approaching, the heat became the challenge! When my flight was scheduled in early morning, the temperature was nice. But by mid-morning the heat took every ounce of energy left in my body. With the heat came the high risk of dehydration. You could drink as much as you wanted, but it was never enough when the temperature soared into the mid-fifties Celsius. And that was the outside temperature. You can imagine how it felt inside a cockpit with no air conditioning.

By the time I closed the doors, started the engines, taxied to the end of the runway and finally received clearance for take-off, up to thirty minutes could pass. Once I got airborne and gained altitude, it cooled down somewhat, but I was often a mess even before starting the first leg of the day. With the plane sitting on the ground and burning under the sun, every piece of metal was so hot you could have cooked an egg on the surface. I would burn myself just by touching the seatbelt buckle. The power levers and the tiller were made of metal, too, so I'd wrap a rag soaked in ice-cold water around them for a few minutes while embarking and briefing the passengers, which cooled them just enough to hold them without burning my hands.

While in cruise though, we could just relax with the autopilot engaged and admire the view. You may think the vast desert is not much to look at, but I find it fascinating. The patterns the sand forms and the colours changing in multiple brown-orange tones depending the time of the day is mesmerizing. The wind forms waves on the surface of the sand. Some areas are rocky and flat, others have huge dunes.

I was sent to a small camp to cover for another pilot for several weeks at the end of the summer in 2008 and was happy to be away from the politics and stress at the main base. I met Rick, a French guy in charge of security at the airstrip, who became my best friend and more. I saw him every time I took off and landed, but he would then disappear. Over those short few weeks, we talked briefly at the foot of the plane a few times, but on my last day there we sat with a coffee and had a longer conversation. That was it, and I didn't think much about it at the time. A few days later, the pilot who replaced me sent a message saying Rick had requested my email address and could he give it to him. I agreed. Rick wrote me the very next day, and we started exchanging messages regularly, getting to know each other from a distance as he was leaving Algeria. It was his last rotation on this contract.

I was heading for Toronto, Canada, for a one week of yearly simulator training. Never liked that simulator box, mostly because it didn't really fly like a real Twin Otter. It took time to get used to flying the simulator before any of the training could start, but it was a good tool for learning, and it refreshed us on the systems of the aircraft well. The training replicated all types of flying conditions and failures that could occur, especially the rare ones we seldom encountered on a real plane. It could be difficult, exhausting work, but at the end of it I returned to the regular job with renewed confidence, having learned something new. That's the beauty of aviation: you never stop learning.

With the end of the year approaching, I was entering my second in Algeria and was placed on a different project in one of the larger camps about an hour's flight from the main base in Hassi Messaoud. I was busy flying six days a week, usually from sunrise to sunset. With the shorter days and the cooler temperatures, it was quite pleasant in the winter despite having to wear a toque and gloves on cold desert nights.

But once the longer hot days of summer would arrive, my day began with a wake-up call at 4 a.m. for flights leaving at daybreak and returning at sunset. Despite the long days, a couple of great co-workers and I often found enough energy to work out at the gym and relax before bed. I kept the same schedule and routine for the remainder of that year.

Once again, spring was just around the corner, which meant we were heralding the arrival of sandstorm season. My life had become monotonous and, sadly, I wasn't enjoying myself. Work was just that—work. Solitude set in once again at home, and I began to feel more and more disconnected from any sort of social life. Rick sensed that and understood. After writing to each other for months and growing closer as friends, stronger feelings began to evolve. We had a lot in common, and we were alike in many ways; we held the same ideas, convictions and life views. We also similarly felt misunderstood by most people. Even though it was mostly a long-distance relationship fuelled mainly via email and instant messaging, we loved talking about our aspirations and could spend hours conversing about anything.

The attraction was physical, of course, but also quite intellectual. Between my work schedule and his, it was very difficult to find time to meet, but the few occasions we managed to, it was obvious that we shared a special bond; it was very passionate. Too good to be true?

It was indeed. After almost a year of chasing each other, our relationship brutally stopped when I discovered he had another girlfriend. I should have known better!

I was back in Hassi in my third year in Algeria, and based out of Red Med, the main camp. I changed clients again and had an enjoyable flight to the south with a challenging airstrip. It was nestled between high dunes, which was a beautiful site but also tricky on windy days. I'd fly in every morning, have lunch at the rig camp, rest and then fly back to base at the end of the afternoon.

I really enjoyed this project as I was working with and for great people. I was even able to have a bit of fun while on stand-by at the rig site. It was the only place where security was loosened at the time. Instead of having to remain inside the fence of the camp, I was allowed to go for a run in the dunes. I loved the challenge of climbing the big dunes, even when it was over forty degrees with the sun beating down on my head. Of course, I made sure to drink plenty of water to re-hydrate myself. It would have been hard to explain why the pilot couldn't work because of heat stroke! I even managed to convince a co-worker and the security officer at the camp to join me at times. Most of them thought I was nuts! It was good fun and recreation.

After three and a half years working on rotation in Algeria and living in France, I was offered a contract in Uganda and with it, a brand new aircraft to work with. The Twin Otter 400 series was coming onto the market, and we got the first one off the assembly line. I couldn't pass up the chance to discover East Africa as well as the opportunity to fly this new plane. Although it was the same model, it had new systems and was totally upgraded with a glass cockpit. With the confirmation that I would be getting this contract, I was already planning a new future for myself.

I said goodbye to everyone I knew in Algeria, my co-workers and the clients with whom I had worked. I enjoyed my five weeks off back home in France, and I felt happy for this change.

Finding shade in the Sahara Desert in Algeria is a must when temperatures can reach well over 50°C, 2008

After lunch at an oil rig most people would go for a siesta. I preferred hiking on top of the sand dunes under a scorching sun

Approaching one of the many oil rig sites
in the middle of the Sahara Desert

CHAPTER 20

RED EARTH

As I stepped off the plane in May 2011, I stopped, closed my eyes and took a deep breath. Ah, yes! This is it! This is the Africa I remember! The aromas filled my lungs, and my body shivered at the thought of being home again. I was always overwhelmed with feelings of belonging to this land of the red earth. I had no idea what caused it, but it happened every time I returned to this part of the world after a long absence.

I had left Entebbe International Airport around three in the morning, so it was almost daybreak. My room in a little lodge was just a few kilometres down the road, and I was looking forward to some rest. As I entered the hotel compound, I recalled the last time I stood on this very same ground. The day I had ferried my plane from Chad after the Sudanese detention, I had spent my first night in this lodge.

After a few short hours of sleep I was awakened by the sound of many birds in the garden. I got up and sat on the front porch of my room. I was too happy to feel exhausted, and that beautiful morning was all it took to convince me to execute my secret project. I would leave France and move right here, to Uganda, as a home base.

I was about to settle in at the crew house with two other pilots and an engineer. The other great benefit of working on one of these projects instead of the main base in Algeria, is that we were on our own. We only had to do the job and report to home office; as long as the work was completed, no questions were asked. I was working in a more relaxed environment, free of the competition and politics that were part of life in Algeria.

Our plane wouldn't be based out of Entebbe Airport, but rather from a small airstrip named Kajjensi that was closer to Kampala. It was a dirt strip sitting on the edge of Lake Victoria, and we were operating under the Air Operator Certificate (AOC) of the aeroclub, as they were our direct clients. We were also to serve another oil operation and still be doing crew changes as in Algeria.

Our base had a "family" feel to it, and once again I enjoyed work without having to get up every morning saying, "Shit I have to go to work!" Instead, it was, "Great, I get to go fly today!" The passion of flying I had lost in Algeria returned, and I loved my job again.

There were three pilots on the project. The client had requested an extra one as back up in case one got sick, as often happened in a place like this. This made our schedule easier even though we were flying six days a week. We would rotate flying two days followed by a day off and so on. We flew to three airstrips on our route in a triangular circuit which had us back at base at lunchtime. We ate at the aeroclub restaurant overlooking the airstrip and swimming pool. It was a beautiful setting with more of a vacation feel than work. This was the best project in the company, and we planned to keep it secret as long as we could, but we knew others would soon try to weasel into it. We managed to keep it under the radar for a while, but not for long.

The airstrips we flew to were located along Lake Albert, and one of them was in the middle of a national park. It was sad to think that an oil company was going to start drilling for oil right in the parkland. But the scenery was just breathtaking: we saw giraffes along the runway, herds of buffalo bathing in muddy waterholes, elephants walking on the shore of the Nile, hippopotamus and huge crocodiles. It was just an amazing sight.

The Nile River, with its source in Jinja on Lake Victoria, enters into Lake Albert first before continuing its course to Sudan. But before entering Lake Albert, its water has to rush through a tight passage in the rocks creating Murchison Falls, one of the numerous tourist attractions in Uganda. The force of the water is tremendous as the gap is less than ten metres wide. Approximately three hundred cubic metres of water per second forces its way through it. Small boats take visitors up-river close to the falls, but I occasionally got to fly over them and downriver at the request of our passengers. Of course, I could never refuse these few extra minutes of flight.

On my days off, I kept busy gathering information about life in this country and began looking for a place to rent. I had to learn what it took to live here safely since I would be doing it on my own. I again recalled the life of Karen Blixen and how I had been so moved by *Out of Africa*. This was *my* chance to live the life I had dreamed of for years.

The five weeks of my first rotation in Uganda went by quickly, which was a good sign. I loved it there, all of it. When I visited the company headquarters a few days after returning home for my annual training and recurrent courses, I discussed my plan to live in Uganda with the flight ops manager and project manager. I wasn't sure how they would react, but my argument was convincing. Return tickets home every five weeks were not cheap, so I thought they would see the savings on travel costs alone I was offering the company. In addition, I would be right there on site even during my time off; I was easily accessible if they needed cover for another pilot.

They agreed but told me I was on my own with no financial assistance on their part. Later on, many of my co-workers thought that the money the company saved on my travel had been applied to my rental home. But they were wrong. To the contrary, I was spending more out of my own pocket than they were because I covered what the company normally provided—food and transportation to work. Even though it seemed unfair, I let it go and didn't care very much. Once my job was done for the day I could just go home and live my life instead of sharing a crew house and feeling like I was still at work. Being on rotation or off rotation converged into a more stable life, as I wouldn't have to pack a bag every other month.

So, I returned to France for my last few weeks. It was a mad dash to get rid of everything I didn't need, settle paperwork and sell my car. Before leaving Uganda at the end of my first tour, I found a perfect apartment and would be able to start my lease on August 1, 2011. Within the next three weeks I said goodbye to friends at the archery club where I'd been taking lessons the past year and to the owners of my condo. I sold my car for the best price I could get on such short notice. Someone got a good deal, but it wasn't me! Finally, I shipped two boxes of personal belongings ahead of my arrival.

I was back on Ugandan soil on July 31, and this time it was for good.

CHAPTER 21

MY *OUT OF AFRICA*

It was busy at work, so I was up and flying on my first day. After work I picked up the keys for my condo, and with the help of a new friend, a single mom who was to be my new neighbour, I went into town to shop for the first basic items I needed. I quickly learned to be patient with the crazy traffic of Kampala. I returned to the crew house after ten o'clock that night, picked up my bags and said goodnight to my co-worker.

I finally opened the door of my new home, a semi-furnished two-bedroom apartment on a hill, and dropped my bags on the floor. I skipped supper in favour of christening my bed with new sheets. I brushed my teeth, put on my pajamas and fell in like a rock, exhausted after a long day.

The next morning, I arose early, enjoyed the view from my balcony for a few minutes and prepared for work. The company minibus would be picking me up until I found a new car. I wanted to be autonomous as quickly as possible, so it only took a few weeks to buy my own ride.

I was on the morning flight every day for the first week. The usual stand-by time after lunch had us sitting at the base until four, then I would return home. I changed from my uniform to civilian clothes then went into town to buy whatever I could carry at one time, until I had everything I needed. My apartment had only the basic furniture, so I had to buy everything else. I also started the paperwork for a residency visa, bank account, water and electricity account and, of course, looked for a small car. Not wanting to disrupt the work schedule, I never revealed how tired I was juggling the job and settling into my new life. It was my own personal challenge, and I wanted to ensure I could do it on my own. And I did.

Rick also loved the disorder and beauty of Africa and had spent many years there as well. A year had passed since our relationship ended, but we had been in touch again not long before I left Algeria. We might not have been lovers anymore, but our friendship and understanding were just too strong to keep silence between us. He had insisted that we meet in person once more before I left France. I was reluctant at first because I was afraid to awaken deep sentiments, but he insisted, and I gave in. I took a night train to Paris, and we met for a few hours while he was transiting to his job posting. We went for coffee, caught up on things and of course, what was meant to happen did happen. I didn't want it to, but the attraction was too strong.

Since I didn't want history to repeat itself, I told him that if we were going forward with a relationship, it wasn't going to end the way it had before. I asked him if he was free this time, and he told me he was. Before leaving, we decided he would come to Uganda soon to visit me. With that, I caught the train and took the eight-hour journey home again. Within twenty-four hours I had travelled eight hundred kilometres back and forth to Paris.

After being settled in Uganda for a few months, Rick flew down to join me and stayed for a couple of weeks. By then I had my own car, a Toyota RAV4, the perfect 4x4 for the African bush. We organized a little vacation, driving from Kampala to Murchison National Park for a game drive to view the wildlife. It took about five hours to reach the park, half of it on bush roads. I was so glad I had a 4x4. We saw elephants, giraffes and all the other wildlife the park had to offer.

We stayed at a beautiful lodge in a cabin overlooking the Nile. With the sound of monkeys in the trees and jumping on our deck, and the hippos below in the water, it was a moment in my life when I felt everything was perfect. We sat with a drink, enjoying the view before the sun went down. There were majestic elephants below the trees on the other side of the river. I watched them for a good hour, mesmerized by their beauty. I was truly living the African adventure I had dreamed of as a kid.

As perfect as all this sounds, I refused to be totally blinded by this relationship and my feelings. Yes, I wanted it to work. Badly. He was the perfect match for me. It was difficult to find someone who understood my lifestyle, and we were so much alike. But I wasn't stupid, and I knew he had his own agenda. He wanted to visit an old friend he had done business with in the past. He said he wanted to thank him for his help at the time and discuss a future project. I couldn't help feeling used, but I accepted it, at least for now. By the end of his stay, I had met his friend as well. He became a good friend of mine, someone I could count on if I was ever in trouble.

A few days before Rick was due to leave, my co-worker Antoine, who was based in the neighbouring country of South Sudan, contacted me. He had booked a three-day vacation out of Entebbe to track gorillas in the Bwindi Forest, one of the major attractions in the country. He had planned to do this with his girlfriend, but something happened at the last minute and she couldn't make it. He had already paid the park fee, $500, which would have been a great loss, so he asked if I was interested in joining him. The timing was perfect. He was due to leave the next morning when Rick was due to depart. "Why not?" I said.

To simplify things, I booked our last night at a lodge in Entebbe where the gorilla tour was to begin. Antoine and the tour guide picked me up in the morning as I was saying goodbye to Rick. I didn't have time to feel sad about it. I was on my way to the west side of the country, to the mountains where the last remaining gorillas lived.

We stopped at the equator and took pictures with one foot in the northern hemisphere, the other in the south. It took over ten hours to reach Bwindi, but the lodge waiting for us was breathtaking. It was peacefully nestled in the forest, and the cool temperature of the higher elevation was a nice change. It was the off-season, so we were the only tourists besides two others. After enjoying a fine dinner, we went straight to bed as the next day required that we be well rested for the hike that would bring us face to face with these magnificent animals.

After an early breakfast, we joined the other members of our group. There were a limited number of permits allocated each day and, with a maximum of eight persons per group visiting one of the nine gorilla families, no more than seventy-two people were allowed to travel to Bwindi each day.

The families were located in various parts of the forest and had become habituated to humans. They never stayed in the same place, building new nests in different locations each night. Another team of rangers was already deep in the forest tracking them from their last known position to where they would wander that day. As we began the hike with our guides, the rangers used handheld radios to communicate where the gorillas were so we could find the right place. How long it would take us to reach them depended on how far the gorillas had travelled. It could take anywhere from one hour to several hours walking through thick bush up and down the side of the mountain in very humid weather. Needless to say, being in good shape made the trek that much easier. They also made sure visitors weren't sick, as gorillas are sensitive and could easily be infected by someone with the flu or other viruses.

We started our hike by climbing the side of the mountain, passing villages and fields of tea. The sky was overcast, as was the case most of the time in these mountains. If you've seen *Gorillas in the Mist*, you know what I mean. I was excited about seeing the gorillas and enjoyed tracking them. When we finally entered the thick forest and arrived where the family was, I was almost disappointed that we had only walked one hour. But when the guide told us to drop our bags, prepare our cameras and walk a few metres more, suddenly, seeing the black, shiny fur of these majestic animals dispelled any disappointment. Just seven metres in front of me was the silverback with a female and a baby sitting at the foot of a tree. Branches were cracking all around us and, when I looked up, I realized the rest of the family was there, too, pretty much surrounding us. They were looking down upon us from the trees while eating some fruit.

We were allowed exactly one hour to observe them, so we all took a position that was as comfortable as possible. The cameras clicked non-stop with everyone taking as many shots as possible. For the most part, each member of the family was going about their usual business. But once in a while, the silverback would look at us. The split-second his eyes made contact with mine was such an emotional feeling. Before our allocated time had expired, the rest of the family descended from the trees, one by one, and gathered around the silverback just a few metres in front of us.

Suddenly, they became agitated and growling like they were saying, "OK, it's time for you to leave." They had been doing this many years, so they knew our hour was up. Our guide agreed, so we took a few last pictures, slowly picked up our backpacks and started walking back out of the forest. Once out in the fields again, we stopped at the edge of the treeline to enjoy a boxed lunch just before the rain started. We still had about an hour's walk ahead of us to reach our cars. As the rain increased, I quickly put on my poncho to cover my backpack.

It began to pour so hard that the trail turned into a river. With our boots getting soaked and water splashing all around us, we were wet to the waist. But it had been a great experience and, still in awe of this close encounter with the gorillas, the rain didn't matter much.

Back at the lodge, it was time for a hot shower, a nice dinner and an early bedtime. The next day, we were back in the car for the trip back home.

Soon after my return to the capital city, I was back at work. I settled into a routine of flying in the morning, working in the office in the afternoon and arriving home at night. There was never a dull moment while living on this continent. If it wasn't a power outage that sometimes lasted for days, it was a water shortage. Then there were the big thunderstorms and the roof leaks in my bedroom and living room.

I had installed a power regulator to avoid damage to my computer and bought a couple of extra batteries that would kick in when the city power went out. But as these outages could last five or six days, they would hardly suffice and were only useful for small electrical equipment. No power meant washing my clothes by hand in the bathtub and throwing away the food in my fridge which, of course, often happened right after filling it; Murphy's Law again! My computer and cell phone batteries died when I couldn't recharge them. All this was a normal part of life in Africa, and I got used to it.

The lack of security was frustrating and unsettling. The guards spent more time sleeping or doing anything other than what they were assigned to do. There were thefts in a neighbouring unit, and a car was broken into in the middle of the night. The thieves were good at it because they managed to bypass the alarm system, break a window to open the car and disable the electrical parts.

One of the worst incidents was when one of my neighbours was woken up in the middle of the night by someone climbing the wall to her bedroom balcony. The intruder entered the bedroom through the window, walked across the room, grabbed whatever he could and simply walked out the main door. The neighbour, a single expatriate woman, was alone that night, and she pretended to be asleep and let the intruder do his thing as long as he wasn't endangering her—probably the safest thing to do to avoid a more dramatic outcome. Luckily, my building had steel bars on the windows and doors, making it almost impossible to enter unlawfully. But still, security issues were always in the back of my mind when living there.

The number of flights at work increased as a second oil company had contracted us. In the morning, I would fly the usual triangular flight, always to the same two airfields. I'd eat a quick lunch back at the base while the aircraft was being refuelled, then I was airborne again about an hour later. First, I had to pick up the passengers at Entebbe airport, a quick five-minute flight from our base. Some days it was difficult to find a parking spot on the ramp at the airport because it was so busy and overcrowded. Waiting for passengers and luggage to arrive easily wasted another hour or more before we were airborne again.

When we were finally onto our destination, an added challenge was that thunderstorms often reached maturity in the afternoon. On the way back it was another stop in Entebbe to drop off another load of passengers. The last leg of the day was more relaxing as we just had to fly back to home base. I loved taking off with the plane so light without passengers and with minimum fuel. The Twin Otter and its ability for short take-offs and landings made it fun to fly. My co-captain and I would often challenge ourselves to see how short and how quickly we could land and stop. Even after having flown that aircraft for years, I still enjoyed every flight as if it was my first.

Landing on a challenging runway or a difficult environment is what makes my job so interesting. We were assigned to check out a new airfield and, after hearing what it looked like, I was definitely on board to get it done. It was shaped like a banana and quite narrow, at least for a Twin Otter. It was south of Lake Albert, and I wanted to see it for myself. My co-captain and our engineer came along for hour-long flight. The different scenery was a nice change from having flown for months to the same location on a daily basis. This region was hilly as it was closer to the Rwenzori Mountains that marked the boundary between Uganda and Congo. Prior to reaching the airfield we had to dive down from a higher plateau because it sat on the bottom of the cliff.

Because it was just a flight to check on the airstrip and no passengers were on-board, the client hadn't set up the perimeter security along the runway. We'd been told there would probably be animals on it, and sure enough, there were antelopes all over the place, so we decided to come in for a low pass to chase them away. Reaching the other end of the runway we pulled up and kept it in a tight turn to return for a landing as quickly as possible. But by the time we were back on final for landing, most of them had returned. We did another low pass from the other direction, once again chasing them away before turning back on final. No luck. Once more they were all gathered in the middle of the strip. It was the only open space in the middle of dense bushes surrounding it, so it was the safest place for them to spot potential predators. After three attempts we decided it was no use and turned around to return to base. We hadn't managed to land, but at least we had been able to check out the airfield and had a good look at it while doing those low passes. When we returned with passengers the next time, security and staff would be present to clear the runway.

My mostly long-distance relationship with Rick grew again in that first year I spent in Uganda. We chatted on the internet or the phone most days. He came to visit again on two different occasions. Each time I booked a three-day trip to one of the parks for a game drive to enjoy the African bush, as I knew he loved it as much as I. We went on a safari with a guide, on foot, and tracked a hyena family to their den. Walking into the bush instead of driving gives a new perspective. We went kayaking on the Nile and spent the nights at a safari camp sleeping in tents overlooking the amazing vistas of Africa. We discussed plans for the future, which even included children.

As he did on his first visit, he met with his friend to discuss potential work, and I had the feeling that something was not right. There were moments when we would be really close and in tune, then suddenly I would catch him staring into the distance as if preoccupied. When he had that look on his face, all I could think of was what happened the first time around. Deep down, I think I knew there was something wrong with this relationship.

But at the same time, I couldn't believe he would do this to me again. Not him! Especially since he knew how much it had hurt me in the past.

He promised that we would soon spend more time together many times and knew this might be my last chance to build a family. I thought he wouldn't waste my time. Rick was more than my lover. He was also my best friend, my mentor. Never before in my life had I felt so close to anyone, Joel included.

So, I wasn't prepared the day Rick ended our relationship. It was a big slap in the face. A year after reconciling, he left me with more questions than answers. He never provided a reason, only that he couldn't continue the relationship at that time.

I was crushed again. My heart had been broken so often that it made me lose all confidence. Throughout my life, people who were supposed to love and take care of me had used me and then turned their backs, not thinking twice about the consequences. Since that day I've built a wall so thick around myself, that I have difficulty trusting and letting others in my life.

I hit rock bottom. But I got up each morning, tired after a long and difficult night, and made sure to put on a smiling face as I walked out the door. I did what I always do when I'm depressed: I threw myself into work to avoid thinking about my personal life. I also started running again as my way of burning off all the extra energy fuelled by anger. Sports and work were my therapy.

CHAPTER 22

KILIMANJARO

Running again was good because it helped prepare me for a great adventure. Antoine and I decided we needed a new challenge, so we booked a six-day trek to Kilimanjaro in February 2013. The itinerary we choose was Machame Route. We would walk about ten kilometres most days, except for day two when we would walk five. Day five was the summit night with over twenty kilometres to cover in less than twenty-four hours at a great altitude.

Getting the gear needed for it proved challenging. My life in Uganda didn't include winter clothes, and I needed a warm sleeping bag. Antoine helped me order everything I needed online. I had it shipped to his home in France, and he brought it to me when he returned to Africa.

We flew to Kilimanjaro Airport and settled in a little hotel for the first night. We met a French girl originally from Cameroon who joined us, and we became a team of three. Together with the three mandatory guides, the porters and the cook, we were ready to tackle this incredible hike. Everyone was excited and looking forward to the trek, but we were also afraid we might not make it to the summit. However, with our guides saying "Pole, pole," we would walk slowly, the rest depending on how our bodies adjusted to the altitude and reduced oxygen.

By the time we left the hotel and drove to the starting point of the trail, it was midday. We soon found ourselves surrounded by hundreds, even thousands, of people. Most were larger groups, their porters lining up to weigh their loads. Strict rules allowed a porter to carry no more than 20 kg each, which was weighed before we were allowed to continue.

It was a very well organized operation. We walked with our guides while the rest of the team went ahead to set up tents and start cooking before we reached camp each evening. After breakfast in the morning, we began our hike again while they dismantled the camp and packed up. Throughout the day they would pass us and have everything set up before we arrived at the next night stop. It was amazing to see how fit these guys were. They climbed at a fast pace every day with those heavy loads two or three times a month.

We walked a gentle hike deep into the lush forest for about four hours that first afternoon. Monkeys playing in the canopy entertained us while we happily talked about what was ahead for the next few days. We went from 5,380 feet at Machame Gate to 9,350 feet at the crowded Machame Camp. Camps were always crowded, but our team found a quiet and secluded area to set up the tents each day. Each hiker had a small tent, the three guides had theirs and there was a bigger one for cooking, eating and the porters' sleeping area.

The food was great, and each meal began with a plate of popcorn and cookies while waiting for the meals to cook. Then it was a bowl of soup followed by rice or pasta with vegetables and meat or fish. They always ensured we drank and ate plenty, even when we didn't feel like it. There were just a few outhouses at the campsites that were not always in good condition so, like most hikers, we just went into the bush or behind a boulder or tree. Every morning and evening we received a small basin with warm water in front of our tents to freshen up. We used it for the first couple of days, but after that it was way too cold outside to think of undressing and putting water on our bodies. We might have been dirty and stinky but everyone else was too. Nobody cared since it would only be six days until we could enjoy a hot shower again at the hotel.

On day two we began hiking in the morning, the plan being to walk for four to five hours. We were scheduled to visit some caves in the afternoon at the next camp on the Shira Plateau. This was done to let our bodies acclimatize slowly to the rise in altitude. We were well above the treeline at 12,500 feet, and the view was amazing. We could see the snowcap of the summit—which still looked so far away!—and the great plains below. Mount Meru still looked quite imposing in the distance. Within fifteen minutes of reaching the camp, it started to rain and didn't stop all afternoon, so we hid in our tents reading a book or just meditating on the experience. Occasionally we would converse, our tents being close to one another.

On the morning of day three we knew that the easy first couple of days were over and the challenge was to begin. We planned to climb to Lava Tower at 15,190 feet by lunch, spend a little time there, and descend back to 13,044 feet to the Barranco Camp. I was so glad to see the sun the next morning because I had washed some clothes and hung them to dry on a line between our tents the day before. The constant rain in the afternoon followed by the cold night meant they—just like our tents—were frosty and as stiff as cardboard in the morning. I clipped them on my backpack when we began our trek and they dried out in the sun.

By midday, we reached Lava Tower, and the clouds were again rolling in and we sat inside the mess tent for soup. Many of us had terrible headaches due to the altitude. I didn't feel well and was concerned that I might not make it to the summit if I was already finding it difficult. I was a bit upset as I really wanted to succeed. Instead of dwelling on it, I tried to focus on walking all afternoon to Barranco Camp. Again, the set-up of the tents provided amazing views. At the foot of the imposing Barranco Wall that we had to climb the next morning, we could look down the mountain and see the lights of a town in the far distance.

After dinner we went right to bed, hoping for a good night's sleep to feel fresh the next day. Unfortunately, that night was my worst of the hike, and I was unable to sleep because of a headache and stomachache. At four in the morning, I couldn't stand it anymore and left my tent to go to the bathroom. They had constructed a new and modern building with a few toilet stalls. It was clean and had lights. Getting out of my tent was agonizing. It was freezing cold, and I had to find my way with a headlamp, climbing a hill to get there. It wasn't pretty, but my stomach started to feel better afterward, and I was able to sleep for a couple of hours.

After a hearty breakfast, the sun came out to warm us on day four, and our little team was amongst the first to get going. Our guides said it would be best to start before everyone else, as once we started to climb the rocks of Barranco Wall there was no way of passing slower groups. A large, slow queue would form there before reaching the top. The face of Barranco Wall is about a one-thousand-foot vertical. Seeing the tiny coloured dotes criss-crossing the wall made me realize how high it was. The path was well defined, and there were a few places where I had to pull myself up—it was a real test. But considering that the porters had to do it with heavy loads on their heads, it looked easy for us.

Once above that ridge we had a little break and took some pictures. This day would be a long one with about an eight-hour hike to reach Barafu Camp. Only the summit remained for the following day—or the coming night, as we would be starting at midnight. We had to circle around the mountain to reach Karanga Camp for lunch. Some groups were taking seven days to do it all so they would stay at Karanga for an extra night of acclimatization. But as we were doing it in six days, we would continue after a healthy meal.

Once again, the clouds started rolling in, and as we began the afternoon hike, they caught up to us coming in from below. A light rain began and quickly turned into ice pellets, as we were gaining altitude again. Surprisingly, I was doing fine after the previous bad day and night. I felt 100% again and was enjoying the hike. Antoine was also doing great. But our new friend was showing signs of struggle due to the lack of oxygen. She had lost her smile and happy temperament, so we were trying to cheer her up as much as possible.

Barafu Camp felt like the moon. Our tents were tucked in between rocks on the slope, and we could catch a glimpse of the snowy peak hiding behind the clouds. We sat around the dinner table in the mess tent enjoying hot soup and dinner. Of course, the tension and excitement were mounting as we were on the last stretch to the summit. The big question, "Are we going to make it?" had nearly been answered. Our guide checked each of us to determine the level of oxygen in our blood. To everyone's surprise, the meter read 100% at my fingertip. My headache was gone, my stomach was fine, and I was feeling great.

At seven o'clock we went into our tents to rest and sleep after this long day. This would be the last sleep we would get for twenty-four hours, but the excitement and adrenaline made it impossible. It was just good to rest my legs and close my eyes for a bit.

Our guides came to our tents with hot tea to wake us up around 11:30 p.m. While we dressed in layers as warmly as we could, the porters prepared breakfast. The altitude had eliminated my appetite, but I forced something into my stomach as I knew I would need as much energy as I could get.

When we left camp, it was almost half past midnight, and most teams had already begun the slow climb into darkness. It was amazing to see a line of small headlamps making its way up the mountain like a snake. It was pitch dark and very cold. We were lucky it was a clear night; no snow and no wind. The plan was to walk for an hour and take a break. We would keep walking with a break after each hour, one foot in front of the other, until reaching the summit. I wasn't too keen on stopping, but I resolved to follow the team and see how it went.

After the first hour we stopped to lean against a big rock and drink some water—or try to! I had brought some sport gel to replenish energy, but I could barely swallow it. I put it away and decided to concentrate on drinking more. As we started walking again all I could see on my headlamp path were the boots of the guide in front of me. We each had our own guide for this summit night, and Oscar was assigned to me. They remained by our side all the way, pushing us to our limits but also checking on our well-being to ensure we were OK. At the first sign of trouble, they would have to decide if it was time to turn back.

Our friend had to stop again after only thirty minutes. She was doubtful, feeling ill and already thinking she might not make it.

We encouraged her, and her guide told her to go slowly and not try to keep up to the others. I was having trouble with the stop and go process. Every time I stopped, I would lose my rhythm and get cold, making it harder to start again. Oscar noticed that without asking me. He'd been watching me for the past five days and knew how I functioned. So that night I didn't have to say anything. In addition, we had already discussed how we were prepared to do everything we could to summit, even if it meant splitting up the group.

"Myriam, do you want to go? We can keep going," Oscar said.

I looked at my friends, and Antoine said, "Go!"

I gave them a word of encouragement, wished them luck and said, "See you up there!"

Oscar and I kept walking and walking. We passed other teams, some of which were going more slowly while others were taking a break. Oscar was very encouraging with his "Pole, pole!" but he eventually had to stop to pee. He was very apologetic. I laughed and said, "Of course, go!" I leaned against a rock and tried to drink more water, but I couldn't. Moving on in total darkness we had to step around vomit that was splashed on the trail from people getting altitude sickness. I kept looking at the boots of Oscar in front and thinking, "Keep walking, breath, breath, breath!" My breath was getting shorter and my steps slower. My nose kept dripping until there was no point in blowing it anymore; it was producing a constant flow of liquid.

Suddenly I had to stop because my heart was racing like crazy. It scared me. Oscar turned around, grabbed me by my shoulders and looked me in the eyes.

"Breathe deeply! Again and again," he said.

When I did, my heart slowed down again. "OK! I'm good!" I said. "Let's go!"

There was a competition in my head between *One more step, one more step. Don't give up. Keep going. Just walk. You can do this. Come on* and *Aaaaah, I can't. I'm not going to make it! No, come on. Keep going. You can do this. You're strong. It's all in your head. Keep walking. Come on. Come on. Come ON!*

It was a real struggle. I didn't want to know what time it was because I think it would have discouraged me, so I kept on walking. It seemed like I'd been walking for hours and it was still so dark. My heart started racing again, so we had to stop one more time. I took deep breaths, but this time the altitude and lack of oxygen hit me harder. According to Oscar I was at about eighteen thousand feet when I started to feel dizzy. I faltered a few times and stumbled but prevented myself from falling. For a moment, I thought I had reached my limit, and I told Oscar so. He grabbed me in his arms and said, "Look! We can see the ice right there. We're almost there! Just a small distance and we're at Stella Point. Take a deep breath, go slow, and you'll make it. You can do it!"

He was just amazing. He knew exactly what to say to keep me going, so I did. I couldn't see the ice. I couldn't see the summit. I couldn't see anything because it was still so dark. But after another very slow thirty minutes, I reached the edge of the glacier. I could see the sign that said, "Congratulations! You have reached Stella Point," which was at 18,830 feet. This was not the official summit yet, and I was surprised I had made it this far with no sign of the sunrise! How long had I been walking?

I began to realize how fast I had climbed throughout the night, so I was motivated. Instead of stopping and taking the usual pictures, we decided to keep going. Oscar told me it would take another forty-five minutes to an hour to reach Uhuru Peak. That motivated me again; I really wanted to make it there for sunrise. I kept walking and, even though I was still feeling dizzy and lifting my feet was getting harder, I pushed myself and actually enjoyed walking the small incline to reach it. Thirty minutes later, I finally saw another sign that said "Congratulations! You are now at Uhuru Peak! 5,895 metres (19,340 feet). Tanzania, Africa's highest point!"

"I made it! I made it!" I said, tears of joy rolling down my cheeks.

Oscar congratulated me and took my picture in front of the sign. Only then did I realize that not only had I made it, but I had done so before sunrise. I was among the first ten people to reach the summit that day! It was 6:30 a.m., and I had reached the summit in just under six hours. Unbelievable!

Daylight was breaking, and after a few more pictures and videos on my action camera, it was time to start descending. For safety reasons I couldn't remain at that altitude very long. It was still quite dark around me as the sun hadn't peaked on the horizon yet, and at that point I was unable to grasp the full extent of my exploit. The lack of oxygen and extreme fatigue was taking all of the energy left in my brain. I slowly walked down from the summit. With the amazing sight of the sun arriving on the horizon there was now plenty of light to enjoy the beauty of the remaining glaciers and the crater of the old volcano. It was breathtakingly beautiful being on the "roof of Africa." What an epic moment!

I came across more people who were still ascending on my way down to Stella Point. I kept wondering if my friends were still climbing or if they had turned back when I saw both of them with their guides. They had just passed Stella Point and were making their way up to Uhuru! I was so happy to see them and so glad they had kept on going.

"You're almost there, guys! Keep going. See you back at camp!"

It was time to start the dreadful descent toward Barafu Camp. Getting there took another three hours shuffling down the coulee in the loose volcanic rock and dust. I never liked the downhill. Or, I should say, my knees didn't! The pain was nearly debilitating, but I soldiered on and finally arrived back at the camp. The cook and porters provided fruit juice to help restore my body's energy. I then withdrew to my tent, flopping on my sleeping bag. I couldn't sleep though. I was overtired and still too excited with what I had accomplished. After lying motionless for an hour, my leg muscles seized while I was attempting to walk to the outhouse. I could barely move with the pain.

Antoine arrived back at camp a couple of hours after me, and our new friend about half an hour after him. They were both exhausted, too, and their bodies rejected the fruit juice. After resting a while, we sat around the table for lunch, then continued our descent soon after. We took a trail that led pretty much straight down the mountain, arriving four hours later at our last campsite. At dinner we discussed the summit evening, reflecting on that amazing experience, laughing at our sore bodies and enjoying the moment. We ended that day early with the best night's sleep we'd had in a long time; it had been three days since that had occurred.

The next morning, we enjoyed our last breakfast and walked the final four hours down this majestic mountain. The minibus awaited us, and we drove to a restaurant to share lunch with our guides, who presented diplomas to each of us.

Our vacation was not yet over though. To provide time to recuperate from Kilimanjaro, we booked a five-day safari in the Serengeti, touring in a 4x4 and camping along the way. We were mainly resting our legs while viewing the wildlife. Throughout Ngorongoro Crater, Lake Maniara and the soaring plains of the Serengeti, I soaked up the beauty and splendour of what the best of Africa had to offer. Ngorongoro is just incredible. A conservation area covering over eight thousand square kilometres includes this amazing crater. It's the world's largest intact caldera and home to an incredible amount of wildlife, including the big five: elephants, buffalo, rhinos, lions and leopards, who are all attracted by the very fertile volcanic grounds.

CHAPTER 23

ETHIOPIA

A week later, I was back home and at work. I wanted to continue my running as I was doing so well before the Tanzania trip. However, I wasn't expecting what happened next. Just a few days after my return, I donned my runners one evening and went out for a jog. As soon as I started running my legs felt extremely heavy, and I had to stop after only one hundred metres. I had no energy and couldn't continue. It was going to take more than just a few days to recover from Kilimanjaro!

Nearing the end of my second year in Uganda, my dream of having a little house of my own and ending apartment living was on my mind. I started looking in the neighbourhood, but the problem was that renting a house was extremely expensive for expatriates and most of them were way too big for only one person. While on my runs in the previous few months, I had noticed a house under construction on the side of a hill. It was eventually completed, and I saw people around it and clothes hanging on a railing, so I thought someone had already moved in.

However, one day when I ran past the property, someone was standing at the gate, so I asked if it was for sale. I was happily surprised to hear that nobody lived there yet because the inside wasn't quite finished. He said it would be completed within the next few months and took me for a tour. It had a steep access road to its lot. The owners had planned to build four houses, one behind the other, each higher than the other in front to avoid obscuring their view. I fell in love with it as soon as I walked in. It was just perfect, the little home I had always dreamed of. I had to do this. After contacting the owners, we discussed the price and move-in date and settled upon two months down the road. That gave me time to plan and get organized.

I finished my rotation at work and planned another trip for my next time off. I was turning forty and decided to make it count. I scheduled a trek to the Simien Mountains, one of the nine UNESCO World Heritage Sites in Ethiopia. This was a two-week trip with half of my time visiting cultural sites in Addis Ababa, Lalibela, Gondar and Aksum, and six days hiking in the mountains. Eight of us hiked all day then set up camp next to small, remote villages. These people lived so far from civilization that it felt like we had stepped back in time. Ethiopia was the most amazing country I'd ever been to, so different. The second most populous country of the continent, it comprises more than eighty different ethnic groups and as many languages. The diversity of the landscape from high plateaus, rugged mountains and deep valleys was formed over ages by tectonic displacement and volcanic eruptions. The majority of the high plateaus sit at two thousand metres and higher, with more than twenty mountains reaching well over four thousand metres. Its highest peak is Mount Ras Dashen at 4,620 m. The people seemed like they were from a different world. Even the wildlife—gelada baboon, Simien fox, klipspringer and others—is indigenous to this region alone.

The cultural and historic sites were as breathtaking as the landscape surrounding it. The Church of Saint George in Lalibela is carved deep down into the rocks and made me wonder how their ancestors managed to create such an incredible building. We visited numerous monolithic churches, each one with its own unique characteristics.

The food was also unique. Injera, a sour fermented flatbread served with most meals, was good, but the sauces that came with it were too spicy for me. I liked spice, but without a gallbladder, I couldn't digest it anymore. Similarly, if I ate red meat my liver struggled to deliver the enzymes needed for digestion. In such cases I could easily end up with a stomachache—or worse—with symptoms of food poisoning. That occurred on the third night of our trek. I started vomiting, and that night was dreadful.

Not wanting to slow down the team, I decided to try and continue the hike the next day. I was weak and tired but wanted to keep going. After fifteen minutes of hiking up toward a mountain, we were close to reaching the highest point of the trek, well over four thousand metres. I suddenly fell to the ground and realized I couldn't continue. My body wouldn't follow my will. The rest of the group and one guide continued on without me for that day, and the other guide remained with me. After ensuring I was comfortable, he walked to the nearest village to hire a man with a donkey.

I dozed off and on in the tall grass until the guide finally returned. I climbed on that cute little donkey, and he carried me for the rest of the day on to the next scheduled campsite where we all regrouped.

When dinner came around, our guide brought me a plate with just plain rice. Thank God! The cook finally understood that I couldn't eat spicy food and realized she needed to set aside plain food for me. I managed to eat some rice, drank as much as I could, and quickly fell asleep.

When I awoke it was already morning. Gosh, that was good. Somehow, I had slept through that night and recovered somewhat from that episode. I was still weak, but I decided to get up and follow the rest of the group who were preparing to continue the trek. We were scheduled to hike up another mountain and, because it would be facing the sun, the guide decided to start the day at five in the morning to avoid the heat. Instead of being near the front of the group as usual during the trek, I was far behind and struggling to keep up. I was pale and still hadn't fully recovered, but I hung in there and kept going. It was the last day of the trek, and I knew I'd be sitting on the bus again the next day. I really wanted to finish it.

We stopped for lunch at a small village in a very remote area that was surrounded by majestic mountain peaks. The rock formations were nothing like I had ever seen, some of them resembling a hand with a finger pointing to the sky. They served us really good food, and I was so hungry. After two days of barely keeping anything down, I asked for a second plate. Everyone was happy to see me doing better and finally getting back on track.

After a few more hours of hiking, we were back on the bus. We discovered someone had rummaged through our bags. We had left some belongings behind that we didn't need on the six-day hike and had been given plastic bags to store our things. We were told they would be safe in the bus with the driver, but all the bags had been opened and searched. Whoever had done this tried to refill the bags, so now our belongings were all mixed up. I found pants, shirts and personal items that didn't belong to me, and my things were found in other bags. The only way to sort this out was to lay everything out on a table and pick our belongings out one by one.

Of course, a few valuable items had been stolen. Our guide was also upset because he had left a bag of money under his seat which had also disappeared! The driver claimed that a thief had raided the bus during the night, but his story didn't add up since the bus was locked and there were no signs of a break-in. Furthermore, why would a thief take the time to put everything back into the bags before leaving! I talked to the guide about my thoughts on the matter, and those of a few others in the group. We wanted to challenge the driver about his story because it just didn't make sense.

One lady had left an empty water bottle behind, but when she picked it up again it was full. As soon as she said that, I thought, *It's not water!*

"Don't!" I said. "I'll bet he pissed in it!"

She looked at me and said, "No! Come on! It can't be!"

She sniffed and exclaimed, "Aaaaaah! It is piss!"

Everyone looked at us with incredulity on their faces, and I was in Agatha Christie mode now.

"There weren't any thieves on this bus," I said like I was cracking the case in one of her books. "It was the driver who probably partied, got drunk and thought it would be fun to check out our bags. When he awoke the next day and realized what he'd done, he put everything back in place—or so he thought. Then, to save his job, he devised this story, making himself out to be the hero."

We let our guide deal with it and settled into our hotel rooms that evening. When morning came, we discovered a new bus and driver waiting for us. The previous driver had been fired after he confessed.

A couple of days later, I was home in Uganda and relieved to have my own food again. I had a busy two more weeks ahead of me before starting my next work rotation. I packed everything I had in preparation to move into my new home. The house was ready, and I had the keys in my hands. The construction crew was still cleaning up around the yard, but I just couldn't spend another day in that apartment; there were too many problems unattended to by the landlord. The electricity had been down every week for so long that it became impossible to keep anything in the fridge. The water supply was also an issue. In the past few weeks, tenants had been lugging water jugs up the stairs, as the pressure in the pump wasn't sufficient. These factors, coupled with the aforementioned security issues, meant it was time to move.

I spent the next day driving back and forth with my little RAV4 fully loaded with bags and boxes. The construction crew used their truck to help me move my washing machine, stove and bed. A day and a half later, I was done! Now all that was missing was the main furniture. The apartment had been partially furnished with it, but I had to buy new stuff for the house. I spent a couple of long days in town searching for what I needed, and instead of going to bigger retail stores I decided to support the local merchants who were building from scratch, on site, and selling their masterpieces along the side of the roads.

Finally, I was all settled and happy to have my own house. No more neighbours. Well, I wasn't really getting away from the noise, but at least I had a little more privacy. Daytime was actually quiet and peaceful. My house sat at the bottom of the property on the side of the hill. It had a garden and a beautiful view overlooking Lake Victoria on one side and Kajjensi Airfield and the Twin Otter parked in the distance on the other side. It was just as I had dreamed.

Back on rotation, the stress increased because I wasn't flying. With things slowing down in the oil and gas industry, we were down to only three flights a week. Having three pilots on duty meant two flights each per week, so I was bored out of my mind. And I wasn't the only one. Some people had too much time on their hands, so they were looking for trouble instead of doing their jobs. I was so frustrated that I showed up at the airfield only on the day that I flew and met the team only once a week for the safety meeting. I spent the rest of the time away from the camp.

Luckily, I received moral support from my South African friends in town. I often drove in to meet them for coffee or lunch during the week, or on weekends they came to my place for a barbecue, or a braai as they called it. They owned a security company and were, of course, concerned about me living alone in a secluded house on that part of the hill. Most expatriates living there were families, and they had installed barbwire fences, and employed a day guard and a night armed guard. I didn't have any of this and couldn't have afforded it had I wanted to. My friends offered me a huge discount on an alarm system for the house, as well as advising me to get a dog.

I'd never had a dog in my life, but a few days later I was at my friends' house looking at beautiful Rottweiler puppies. Maybe it wasn't so much for security, as the pups were still too young to provide it, but more for company so I wouldn't be alone. By the end of the day, I was driving home with the cutest and smallest pup of the litter. I named her Roxy, and she became what mattered most in my life at that time.

ETHIOPIA

Almost another year passed where I kept working on and off doing my rotations, spending most of my free time with Roxy. I had fun training her and was proud of how clever she became. She was definitely protecting me, even at her young age. Anyone coming too close to the compound had to deal with her first. But with me she was just a big baby, and we enjoyed our daily walk or running and playing around the house until we both dropped. She was my girl, my best friend, but what was coming threatened to break my heart again.

I was subject to jealousy and bullying at work. I still enjoyed being in the cockpit, but every other aspect of my job was filled with negativity, and I'd been dealing with it quietly by myself for too long. I had been able to handle it, fighting back to maintain my position and do my job. However, the trouble became so serious that I burned out. When I finally admitted my shoulders were not broad enough to carry this kind of load on my own, I had to make one of the most difficult decisions of my life. It was time to take a break from all of this and move on. Once again, I'd leave everything I had built, but after thinking it through, I had no choice but to take yet another leap of faith if I wanted to survive and maintain my health and sanity. It was time to return to Canada.

I set a plan in motion to make this transition as smooth as possible, knowing it would not be easy. I was already physically and mentally weakened, so this wasn't the time to make a mistake. First off, I decided to take a three-month unpaid leave from my company to give me the summer to move across the ocean and settle back in Canada. I also knew I would leave that job, too, as the stress was the main reason for my departure from Uganda.

I started looking for other potential interesting work. While in the process of selling what I owned in Uganda, I contacted a real estate agent in the Vancouver, Canada area. I wanted to return to the province I knew best, and also where my brother was settled. I was determined to buy a condo and have a place of my own; no more rentals while paying off other peoples' mortgages. It was time to invest and have a place of my own.

Selling my car and furniture was not an easy task in Africa. As a single woman, I was an easy target for crooks and thieves. I knew it; I'd been around the block long enough to know how things worked. But despite having done everything possible to be careful, I couldn't keep my worst nightmare from occurring.

I had to let strangers into my compound to view what was for sale. Though I always tried to have someone around the house during this time, I was alone one particular day. A gentleman in a suit and tie drove up with someone he claimed was his driver. He presented himself as a businessman from the war-torn neighbouring country of South Sudan and was starting a new business in Uganda. He said he had just bought a house and needed to furnish it. He liked what I had and pretty much wanted to buy everything.

"I'm here for another month and will still need most of it," I said. "But I can put it aside for you with a deposit."

He agreed, though he wanted a few things right away. We settled for a few items that I wouldn't need anymore that would fit in their car. He paid me in US dollars and agreed to return the day after with a deposit for the rest. He even said he would probably buy my car as well.

I had an uneasy feeling. It was too easy, something was not right. I didn't want him to notice my suspicion and place myself in a compromising situation while alone, so I just smiled and let them go with the few little items. As soon as they left, I grabbed the cash he gave me, jumped in my car and drove to the bank.

"Are these bills counterfeits?" I asked the teller.

"Yes, they are!" she said, unsurprisingly.

She advised me to file a report with the police, so I did.

They sent an officer back home with me, so they could see where I lived, as the thieves were supposed to return for the rest of the furniture. That would make an easy arrest! But wait a minute. This is Africa. If I charged them and those guys were arrested, how long do you suppose they would remain in jail? This was a country where police were so underpaid that corruption was at its worst. Charging them would be like signing my own death warrant because if they didn't come find me, their friends would.

I grabbed my phone and dialed the number of that "gentleman." I told him I knew his money was fake, and that I wanted my things back. I didn't really, but I wanted to scare him away so he wouldn't return and let him know I wasn't stupid and wasn't playing his game. It worked because he hung up on me and disconnected that number. I had maybe lost a couple of hundred dollars of furniture, but at least I was alive. I just had to sell the rest of my belongings and quietly get through one last month.

The hardest part was dealing with Roxy. I looked into every possible solution. I wanted to keep her with me, but even if she survived the long trip, there was no way I could keep her in Canada because I had no idea how things would unfold for me. Would I find a place where they accept her breed? How could I keep her in a small condo in a city after she had so much freedom in Uganda? What would I do with her while on my work rotations?

Every solution I could think of to keep her was not fair to her. I could have given her back to my South African friends, but I knew she would end up in a kennel with her siblings and become a guard dog. Stuck in a cage all day long, she would be brought to random houses for night security. I didn't want this for her, not after the life I had given her.

In the end, I finally found a family who wanted to take her in. They had a young daughter and three other dogs. At least she would have new friends to play with and be well cared for. It was very difficult to let her go, and I'll never forget the look on her face the day they came to pick her up and we had to say goodbye. Ever!

An unsuccessful landing on a new runway at the south end of Lake Albert, Uganda. After three attempts at chasing the antelopes away, we had to abort

On the equator. One foot in the north, one foot in the south. Uganda, 2011

Giving my passengers a scenic tour of Murchison Falls, Uganda

CHAPTER 24

NEW JOB, NEW LIFE

In May 2014, I stepped down from the plane in Vancouver, Canada. My brother and his girlfriend welcomed me back and invited me to stay with them until I found a place of my own. I didn't want to waste time, so on my second day there I was already running to various offices to reactivate my resident status, driver's license, bank account and so forth. Keeping myself busy was the only way I knew how to cope with this huge change and the loss of my girl Roxy. By the end of the first week, I had all my paperwork in order, had bought a little car and booked an appointment with the real estate agent to view a potential new home.

Weeks went by as I was resettling into my life in Canada. It was a strange feeling after all those years away from it, but it also felt very good to rest. I enjoyed the freedom of walking anywhere I wanted without needing eyes on the back of my head all the time.

A company that completed survey work in Twin Otters contacted me for an interview, so I flew across the continent to North Carolina and met with the chief pilot. I loved what I saw. It was a small company with exciting work, exactly what I was looking for. The interview went well, and I flew back home with the promise that a final decision would be forthcoming.

I received a message from my present company asking me to return to work prior to the end of the three-month unpaid leave. I tried to explain that I needed the extra month as I was in the middle of purchasing a home, but they insisted. I stood my ground and told them the best I could do was to return in two weeks, but they weren't about to give in.

I received a termination letter, effective the following day. Because I was on an unpaid leave, I could be let go on short notice without receiving the two months' termination pay of a full term. After giving seven years of hard work and dedication, the people who wanted me out had received their wish just like that. You'll probably not guess what my reaction was to this. Amazingly enough, I felt relieved! I can't describe it. All the stress and weight on my shoulders lifted within seconds of receiving the news.

Despite my relief I was still left in a potentially difficult position as I had just completed the paperwork for a mortgage with the bank based on having a job to cover it. I didn't care. All I knew was that the nightmare was over.

Life got brighter the very next day when I received a call from the company in North Carolina to offer me the position. I had spent less than twenty-four hours without a job. Incredible. Time to celebrate! Talk about a new life; there wasn't anything more I could have done to make this move a complete life change situation within three months.

Before winter arrived, I was settled in my new home, and after another trip to North Carolina for indoctrination training, I was ready to start this new adventure. I was on stand-by for my first contract, and there were a few different places I could have been sent. In the end, they needed me as soon as possible in Niger. At first the client didn't want a female pilot on that project because it was a small and very remote camp. They were concerned because living conditions were very rudimentary. But once they knew this was nothing new to me, I was assigned for my first mission. I had just a few days to complete the paperwork for my visa and book a flight—not an easy task approaching the holiday season, but I made it work.

This was how I spent my first Christmas back in Canada—in airports travelling from Vancouver to Niamey, Niger, the beginning of yet another adventure. A new life was the best Christmas present I could have received.

CHAPTER 25

FERRY FLIGHT

Returning home after eight weeks in the middle of the Niger desert was a welcome R&R. I had a great time working out there on this new assignment, the team was outstanding, and I was enjoying my job once more.

I did need some rest, though, as the accumulation of fatigue and the limited possibilities of cooking fresh food while at camp so far away from anything had taken a toll on my digestive system. Let's just say that I won't be eating any canned green beans for a very long time! I think I ate enough for a lifetime in those eight weeks.

I had to go back to North Carolina to get yet another check ride for my license during my time off. Even though this type of aircraft doesn't require a type rating in the USA, I was flying it at a restricted weight that was quite a bit higher than the maximum, the same way the military were allowed to. The training was a no-brainer for me, and after a few flights along with my colleagues who had to do the same, we passed our exams and celebrated at a nearby pub before we all headed back to our respective homes to rest up.

While one of the aircraft was heading to Asia and another one to South America, I was heading for a project in Kenya. But first, I had to join my team in Malta where our aircraft was in maintenance and patiently waiting the go-ahead for the next contract.

Malta, one of the seven islets forming an archipelago, stands at a strategic place in the middle of the Mediterranean Sea between Europe and Africa. The capital city, Valletta, was actually the first planned city in Europe, sketched out back in 1565. It showcases a lot of world-class architecture from baroque cathedrals to Greek Byzantine structures. Interestingly, the island does not have one single forest.

Sadly, I didn't have time to play tourist and visit Malta. Upon my arrival we put ourselves to work quickly to get everything ready for our ferry flight. We were to bring the aircraft from its "resting" location to the next where a survey was scheduled. It meant crossing multiple countries and sometimes continents to reach the next destination. We made sure everything was running smoothly on the aircraft, loaded the kit that would sustain us for the duration of the project, and planned each leg for the multiple-day flight.

We left Malta behind early one morning, and flew our first leg over the Mediterranean Sea, heading east toward the Greek Islands. Our first stop was Heraklion. We spent a very pleasant evening strolling the pedestrian streets and enjoying a great meal at one of the multiple restaurants where tourists were enjoying themselves after a long day of sun and fun.

After a good night's rest we departed very early, which was a routine we needed to keep all week if we wanted to stay on schedule. Heading southbound, we crossed the Mediterranean and followed the Nile to our next fuel stop in Cairo. As we arrived over this incredible city my impression was—how can I put it?—very brown. Between the thick haze created by pollution and a city that didn't really provide much of vegetation, every building looked the same from up high. I was thrilled to just make out the famous pyramids sitting on the edge of the city, with the sandy desert right behind them. Cairo was only a quick stop with just enough time to refuel the aircraft and empty our bladders. Off we went again, continuing our journey south.

Our night stop for this second day was Luxor. And what a night! The company sure treated us well during those ferry flights, and we were staying in the best hotels we could. I sure wasn't used to five-star treatment, but I wasn't complaining!

"So…Guys! Want to go for a stroll and explore this ancient civilization's sites a little?"

That was my wish and hope, though it would not happen. Company protocol was tight on our safety and security, so I was put on a short leash and didn't get any opportunity to wander far from the hotel and airports.

The next day had us heading to a country I thought I'd never set foot in: Saudi Arabia. We headed east from Egypt—yes, east, not south, which would have been the fastest route toward Kenya. For political and security reasons we were not allowed to fly over Sudan, so we had to go around it. The only way was to cross the Red Sea to Saudi Arabia and follow the coastline until we could cross westbound toward the Horn of Africa. Oh, we also had to avoid the waters controlled by Syria.

Our first overnight stop was in Jeddah. Oh boy, I sure felt out of place! The rules and beliefs of how women need to be handled and treated there are so far away from mine; I just could not understand it. Needless to say, I had quite a few unfriendly looks come my way just walking from the airport to the taxi and from the taxi to the hotel room because my head was not covered. I was dressed in my pilot uniform. Yes, I know…not the usual sight out there for a woman. But we were meant to stay just that one night, so after a quick meal at the hotel restaurant with my team, I went back to my room and stayed in while they went out for a little fun.

The next morning I made myself as small as I could, jumped in the taxi and went back to the airport to continue our journey.

"Aircraft refuelled? Check! Flight plans filed? Check! Pre-flight? Check! Company called? Check! OK boys, time to roll!"

I felt more comfortable as soon as we were airborne and leaving Jeddah. This first leg of the day took us south over the highlands, a very arid landscape. We were planning to land in Jazan at the southwest corner of Saudi Arabia to refuel and continue back to the African continent. We were about halfway through our flight when Control contacted us. Without any explanation, they asked us to turn back and return to Jeddah.

"Wait, what!?"

After confirming the request and making sure we understood correctly, we made a 180-degree turn and headed back north. We received no explanation about why we couldn't continue; we just had to comply. We called our operation room back in the USA via our satellite phone to explain what was happening, have them organize the logistics on the ground and have our contact waiting for us once more in Jeddah.

Just like that, I found myself checking in at that fancy hotel again and keeping my head down. I wasn't sure if it was the men or the women who stared the most. Not wanting to spend the rest of the day stuck in my room, I went to one of the shops inside the hotel, bought myself an idjab and quickly put it on in my room. When my co-pilot texted me to say they were going out to eat, I texted: "Wait, I'm coming too!"

"Well, OK," he said.

They were probably a little concerned, but they had no idea that I was fitted properly for the occasion this time. When I came downstairs, they only recognized me when I was standing right in front of them. They appreciated the effort and smiled.

"Please, no comment," I said. I wasn't feeling comfortable in it. "Let's go eat!"

The reason we were not able to continue our flight the previous day was because there were some bombings across the border in Syria. Our intended airport in Jazan was closed that morning because of the military operation. If we wanted to leave Jeddah, we had to work out a different plan. Our only option was to fly southwest across the Red Sea again to Djibouti where our next fuel stop was scheduled. Even with the extra ferry fuel tank filled up, it was quite a stretch, and we would only be able to make it if the wind conditions were favourable.

After compiling all the weather information, we decided to give it a try. We were in the air early morning and made quite a detour over the water to avoid the Syrian airspace; this was not helping us. But we kept going, keeping our eyes on the fuel gauges and constantly recalculating our endurance and fuel remaining. When we approached the point where we had to decide to continue or turn back, we were fighting against stronger winds than expected. We looked at each other and finally had to admit we were not going to make it across at this speed. Bummer! Once more, we were returning to Jeddah.

"BOHICA!"[1] I screamed in the headsets.

My co-workers burst out laughing even though they weren't too happy either. We were losing days on our schedule to arrive in Kenya, and we were all anxious to get there. All we could do was sit and wait until we could work out an authorization to land in Jazan for refuel before crossing the Red Sea. Our logistical support worked hard for us, and we finally received the green light for the next morning. After one last night in Jeddah, we were finally on our way. This time we managed to make it without being turned around for any reasons.

Following a quick stop in Jazan to refuel, we were back in the air. After flying across the Red Sea and some desolate landscape, we finally found ourselves on final approach to Djibouti. Ironically, this time the guys were not comfortable there, but I found myself right where I belonged. I was so happy to be back on African soil. Speaking French was also a big help while conversing with the locals in the street and at the hotel where we spent the night. It wasn't a five-star hotel here, but I found it charming. The hallways leading to the rooms made me feel as if I was on an old cruise ship.

After a restful night, we set out very early in the morning. We had a long day of flying ahead of us, but we were excited to finally be progressing. If all went as planned, we'd be in Nairobi by evening. The flight took us over the high plateau of Ethiopia, and I recalled exploring the Simien Mountains on foot a few years back. This

---

[1] BOHICA: "Bend Over, Here It Comes Again"

time I got to see it from above, and those arid plateaus and deep valleys were as majestic as they were from the ground. We had to keep climbing to clear some of the ridges, and it was a slow and painful climb for our heavily-loaded aircraft. We barely managed to level at twelve thousand feet. My co-captain was struggling to breathe at that altitude. I was a bit concerned, but he smiled and said he'd be OK.

"You got to stop smoking," I said.

At that moment he couldn't agree more. Hypoxia is felt that much more when you are a heavy smoker.

Soon enough I could see the buildings shaping Addis Ababa. After landing, I taxied out to our parking following the marshaling instructions given to us. Oddly, they asked us to pull in as any other airliner would. *Well, that's going be interesting for departure! Are they going to push us back too?* I thought. We all looked at each other and thought, *This is going to be fun!*

We refuelled to the maximum one more time, had a pee break, bought some sandwiches, got our flight plans and weather for the ultimate leg of this journey, and soon enough we were ready for departure. We asked the grounds crew how we would be pushed out of the parking and, of course, they had no idea. They were not equipped for this type of aircraft, and there was nothing they could do. They all just stood there with blank stares on their faces.

It looked like we'd have to push it out ourselves. The aircraft was fully loaded and definitely not light. On top of it, there was a slight slope to go against. The only option was for me to jump into the cockpit, start the engines and use reverse to make the aircraft move, but even with the help of the engines, I was not able to make it roll backward. The guys jumped back out, and while

I was using as much power in reverse as I could, they pushed. It must have been an unusual sight because a crowd formed around us. They were fascinated.

With the team back on-board, I taxied into position, and we were ready for departure. Applying max power, the aircraft started rolling and accelerating to take-off speed. It took me way more distance than I had expected, and we used a good part of the twelve-thousand-foot runway before I was finally able to get airborne.

The initial climb out was very interesting to put it mildly. The stall warning was telling me I was right at the limit of my speed, and yet I was barely gaining any altitude. All I could do was make sure I didn't go below that speed and hope it would finally accelerate so I could start climbing out. It was definitely not a good feeling to see the high plateau surrounding us while we were still trying to climb. When the control tower called and asked if I could accelerate my climb due to traffic, I had no choice but reply with, "Negative! I'm doing the best I can here!" The controller understood we were not able to gain altitude faster, so he simply let us continue at our own ability and made sure he cleared surrounding traffic accordingly.

At least we were enjoying the scenery that was slowly turning from semi-desert to savanna and rainforests filled with rivers and lakes nourishing more fertile lands. Soon enough we found ourselves crossing the border into Kenya. The landscape would just get more and more beautiful, very green. We even saw a few active volcanos. We were flying along the escarpments marking the Great Rift Valley. No doubt those luxuriant forests were hiding countless wildlife. The weather was changing quickly with thunderstorms building up. One of them even forced us to divert thirty miles off course to avoid it. The size and power produced by storms in this part of the world is just something you don't play with.

At the end of this beautiful flight, Nairobi was finally in sight. Nature gave way to a vastly spread-out city, so it was just a matter of finding that little airport we were supposed to go to in the midst of the buildings, though we knew the runway was on the edge of the city with one side touching a national park. We finally spotted it about ten miles away, so we just had to avoid the heavy traffic around it. We received instructions to slow down and place ourselves behind other incoming traffic two miles ahead of us. This airport was used by an aeroclub and school, so many small aircraft were just practicing take-offs and landings, making circuits around the airfield. Once on the ground, I was just amazed by the number of aircraft parked in every little corner of that airport—obviously way more than an airfield of that size could handle. What a mess!

We first had to clear customs with the aircraft. We were taken to our accommodation that would become our home away from home at least until we started our survey work out east. The drive from the airport to our apartments reminded me of Kampala in Uganda. It was the usual chaos of pedestrians, motorcyclists and more cars and trucks than those roads were meant to handle.

We settled into a daily routine. Every morning we left our apartment and drove to the airport. The survey system on-board the aircraft was complex and required to be plugged in to a power outlet 24/7. We completed a daily check to make sure it didn't turn off due to power failure or someone tripping on the long power cords that were running from the building to the aircraft.

After that, we would drive to the nearby shopping mall and settle on an outdoor patio at a coffee shop for lunch. Afternoons were spent at our apartments. Once again, we were put under tight leash due to the security company's protocol. I was annoyed by that. Having lived three years in the neighbouring country of Uganda,

I was very familiar with East Africa and sure didn't felt the need to be watched over constantly.

The days turned into weeks, and we were still not getting the green light to start our survey work. We managed to organize a little game drive at the nearby national park one day, and a visit to Sheldrick Wildlife Trust, an elephant rescue and wildlife rehabilitation program, on another.

I found out about a museum in the house where Karen Blixen had lived and managed to get a driver to take me. The house itself is not the one seen in the movie as it was filmed in a different location, but it was filled with some of the furniture and clothes used during the filming of *Out of Africa*. This was the real house, the one where Karen Blixen had lived in. It wasn't busy that day, and only a handful of people were visiting it, so I was able to spend as much time as I wanted in each room. A young lady told me stories and facts about the house. I felt quite emotional walking in and around it. I had wanted to see it since I was a teenager, and I lived my own little *Out of Africa* life when I was in Uganda. Imagining how it must have been in Karen's time made me very nostalgic for an era I wish I had known. Once I finished the little guided tour, I sat in the garden, as she probably did, looking at the distant Ngong Hills. What an amazing life she led.

A few days later, our relief crew arrived. We handed over the aircraft and the project to them with mixed feelings. We were happy to go home after eight long weeks but disappointed we didn't get to fly more and begin the survey. We also learned that the go-ahead finally arrived for the following week, meaning that by the time our off-duty tour was over, this survey would be finished, and we would not be returning to Kenya ourselves.

Not knowing what would be next was part of the fun about this job. There would always be a new adventure waiting that could take us anywhere in the world. For now, it was time to head back home, and it was a perfect time to be in Canada. It was full-on summer, and I had great plans about how to spend the next few weeks.

CHAPTER 26

SLEEPING WITH BEARS

I had been living in Canada again for a year, and I was full of energy and happier than ever before. It was the summer of 2015, I loved my new job, and life in British Columbia—where so many outdoor activities were accessible—was so enjoyable. I was already doing a lot of hiking, but this summer, I wanted to get into long hikes and overnights in the alpine. Of course, I'd need the gear, so my first stop was the outdoors sports shops. They were so dangerous for my wallet!

I already had hiking boots and most of the clothing, and I had brought the sleeping bag I used on the Kilimanjaro trek back from Africa. But I still needed a cooking stove, water filter, a light solo tent, a sleeping pad and a pack big enough to carry it all. Based on the distance and elevation I wanted to hike, my goal was to keep the pack to essentials and not overload myself, as I'd be carrying it all on my own.

It was time to explore my new backyard! Garibaldi Provincial Park is an incredibly beautiful backcountry that offers multiple hiking trails, and it is just outside Vancouver. The first one I picked was Elfin Lakes, an eleven-kilometre hike to get to the campground. I'd set up my tent and unload part of my gear, then spend the afternoon hiking farther up to Opal Cone before returning to Elfin Lakes for the night. This was my very first solo overnight hiking trip, and even though I was well prepared and a veteran in the mountains, I couldn't help but feel a bit uneasy. There was one thing I never had to account for when growing up in the Swiss mountains: bears! Part of my gear was definitely bear-spray and a survival kit. I had learned how to make a good one myself while roaming in the African bush.

I left early enough to beat the city traffic, and it would still take me a couple of hours to join the trailhead. Once leaving the edges of the city, it's a beautiful drive north with mountains to one side and water to the other. I was following Howe Sound, where I could see a few islands in the distance. The last portion of the road was dirt, which was rough on my little car. I swore that as soon as I could afford it, I would get myself a 4x4.

I purposely chose mid-week to avoid the weekend crowds. There were only a handful of cars in the parking lot, so I knew I wouldn't see many people. At first, I walked along a large uphill path in the forest, but soon enough I emerged into the alpine with more open views. I didn't see anyone for over an hour on the trail until I crossed paths with a couple of hikers going down.

The trail was beautiful, at first following a logging road, but once reaching the alpine it opened to meadows full of wildflowers. Even though the views were choked by a thick layer of smoke from forest fires, I could still make out the contours of the majestic mountains surrounding me. British Columbia was deep into fire season, and one was burning north of my location. The wind pushed the smoke toward Vancouver. This was probably another reason there weren't too many people hiking at the time, but I didn't want to let a bit of smoke stop me from enjoying our beautiful nature.

After a few hours of hiking, I found myself overlooking Elfin Lakes. There were two gorgeous little lakes with a cabin tucked away in the trees next to them. What a beautiful sight! I quickly found the wooden pads of the backcountry campground. There were plenty to choose from as only two were used already. I set my bag down on one of them and had my tent set up in ten minutes.

With that done, I took a little break, had a sandwich and rested for a few minutes. But there was no time to waste if I wanted to reach my goal and return to camp before dark. I left all the gear I didn't need in my tent and put the essentials for the afternoon in my backpack.

I followed the excellent trail system Park Canada had in place. It was very warm that day, and I was getting thirsty. My water bottle was quickly getting close to be empty, but I had my filter and thought I'd just fill it up again along the way. I knew I was to follow a river so there was plenty of water to take from the mountain. What I had underestimated was that the torrent was big, strong and full of sediment coming down from the snow and glacier melting higher up. It was still early summer. There was no way I could get down safely to the edge of the river, so I just had to keep going and hope I'd be able to filter some water from the lake I was looking for.

That was a good lesson for me because that afternoon hike was much longer than I had anticipated. I thought I'd see the lake after every corner I turned on the trail, but nothing. I kept walking and walking, dehydrated, hot and tired. When I finally arrived, I fell on my knees, filled up my water bottle, and didn't even enjoy the location because it was already time to hike back down to my campsite.

Arriving at my tent I was way too exhausted to even feel hungry. I had overestimated my physical strength and told myself I would pick a shorter hike or give myself more time next time. To add to the discomfort, the bugs were relentless, especially the mosquitoes, so it was simply impossible to sit outside and enjoy a relaxing evening looking at the sun going down. All I could do was tuck myself inside my little tent, lay down on my sleeping bag and just enjoy the moment. I had walked a little more than twenty kilometres that day, and I was ready for a good night's rest.

I realized that the people I had seen midday were gone. Strangely enough, I was all alone. There was not another human around for my first night camping solo in the wild. I'm not going to lie: I was not 100% comfortable even though I had read that the first time is usually a strange feeling before one gets used to it. It becomes easier after that.

The temperature was so warm the inner shell of my tent was enough and I didn't have to put on the rain cover. This gave me a good view of my surroundings, though in the pitch darkness of the night, I couldn't see much. Of course, I didn't sleep that well. Every little noise around me made me jump.

What's that? Something is moving right outside my tent. Is it a bear? Don't move…play dead! Oh man. Is this supposed to be fun?

After a long and mostly restless night, I woke up just before daylight and watched the beautiful colours changing on the mountains surrounding me. It was quite a moment. I checked around the tent and there were no tracks of any beasts. It was probably a little chipmunk or something similar that was looking for my bread crumbs. Silly me!

Once the sun arrived, I went to the lake to wash up before getting my breakfast. The campsite was nicely organized with outhouses, a shelter where people could sit at a table inside if needed, and also those poles with cables along them where you'd hang your food bags out of reach of animals. Clever.

The morning was quiet, and I took my time to relax before packing my gear. I had to get back on the trail before lunchtime and hike the same way back to my car. If I got on the road early enough, I could beat the evening traffic through the city. It was the weirdest feeling being back in the madness of rush hour and back to society. It was only two days, but I felt like I was gone for so much longer.

When I arrived back home by end of day, I was dirty, sweaty, hungry and tired. But I had a stupid smile on my face that I couldn't erase. I felt so happy and so proud of myself. I was definitely hooked, and I knew right in that moment that this would not be my last solo trip.

The following day I stayed home and recuperated by studying maps and books about my next adventure. I had a few weeks ahead of me before I was supposed to go back to my next work rotation, so I fully intended to do one overnight hiking and camping trip every week. And I did.

I gained knowledge of those mountains, confidence and physical strength after each trip, and the uneasy feeling of being alone in the wilderness went away quickly. All that remained was excitement, happiness and a deep feeling of belonging out there. I enjoyed it so much I found it harder and harder to return home. I even extended some overnights into a three- or even four-day adventure all by myself in the most beautiful scenery I could have dreamed of.

And yes, I did come face to face with a bear—more than once. I actually crossed paths with three of them on the same day. Early one morning, I bounded around a corner of the trail and found myself staring at a grizzly cub eating blueberries. I'm not sure which one of us was more startled, but he felt at ease very quickly and went back to eating the berries. I knew Mom wouldn't be that far away, so that scared me the most. I wasted no time getting out of there.

Later that afternoon while I was hiking down the mountain, I saw the mom a good two hundred metres away. My knees started to shake a bit. As I was in a very popular park, I knew the bears were acclimated to humans, but they are still wild animals and you never know. Proper behaviour from humans is also required to prevent problems.

When I arrived back at camp, which was full that day, there was a black bear right along the edge of the campsite. Funnily enough, as I walked toward my tent, I asked a group of people whether they had seen any bears. They said no, and that they were disappointed.

"Just walk ten metres this way and you'll see one!" I said.

That was the best summer of my life, and I wish it would have lasted forever. But, as always, when my life finally seems perfect and when I'm feeling happy about every aspect of it, there's got to be something to come to break it all for me. Sometimes it feels as if I've been cursed.

CHAPTER 27

BAPTIZED BY FIRE

Over the previous few weeks, the oil and gas industry had been suffering, which meant the prospecting had slowed down tremendously as well. It was so slow that there were no more surveys happening, and the client my company was working for went bankrupt. They started by putting projects on hold and were hoping to get back to normal operations. There were eight pilots dedicated to those survey projects. Some were full-time employees and a few of us were independent contractors as we were not US citizens. Over the weeks, the company had to let some pilots go, but they kept saying they wanted to keep me. They held out as long as they could hoping for the best, but in the end they had no choice. They could not use me for other work in country, and those overseas contracts were definitely over.

Just like that, my dreams were shattered again. Back to square one and time to convert my licenses yet again. As I was living in Canada, it was time to get the Transport Canada air transport pilot license (ATPL). I signed up for an online course to study all the important subjects, and this helped me to stay focused and on track. It takes a lot of self-discipline to study alone at home. For two months, I did nothing but sit at my desk and study day in, day out. When I felt ready, I wrote those dreadful exams and passed. One good thing down.

After I sent in my application, I realized I still had to do a check ride on an aircraft. My last check just a few months previous was not approved as it was not done in Canada. Sadly, it's all about money. What frustrated me the most is that once you get hired by a company, you usually have to do a check ride to get on the line anyway, and that check ride could count for what I needed to do for my license. But most companies want you to have the full license before they hire you.

I really couldn't afford to pay for a few hours of training and a check ride just to get this done, so I took a gamble. I started sending my resume out to all the companies I could think of and for which I would enjoy working. I hoped one company would look at my experience and see that I was just thinking logically, so they wouldn't be scared to take the risk. It was November, and I knew nothing much would happen in the following few months as it was winter. Aviation in Canada is very seasonal, and most companies hire in the spring.

So I lived on my savings and was very careful with my spending once more. I would go for walks in the forests, but even if I tried very hard to stay positive, I ended up feeling quite depressed. *Why did I leave my beloved Africa?* It was a tough time again. I would sit on a rock somewhere, anywhere along a trail overlooking the valleys, and cry my eyes out. But I was determined to make it through and see the better times on the other side.

Weeks went by. Then months…

Then, out of the blue I got a phone call from a company I thought was a longshot because I had been (wrongly) told that no women were working in that field.

"Hello, Myriam. Can you come for an interview tomorrow?"

Oh my Gosh! I pinched myself. I better not screw this up. This is my ultimate dream—that one thing left on my "to do list." It was an experience that every pilot dreams of.

I barely slept that night. I was too excited, and I lay awake thinking very hard about what they might ask and how I would answer. Also, I had to explain the issue with my license.

The chief pilot and the ops manager greeted me at their office the next morning at ten o'clock. The meeting lasted about an hour as we discussed different topics, including the fact that I needed that check ride to be issued the final Canadian license. Normally an interview would end with a quick flight in one of their aircraft so they could see how good or bad a pilot the candidate is. But this didn't happen for me, as they needed to review and discuss my case amongst themselves.

I didn't have to wait long, as the chief pilot called that same evening to ask if I could return the next morning to do that flight. They hadn't made a decision yet, but they still wanted to take me up to check on my flying skills.

The next morning, I jumped into the captain's seat of an aircraft type I had never flown before. With the instructions of the chief pilot by my side, I got the engines started and got us airborne. Heading toward the mountains, he asked me to go low and enter a valley. I manoeuvred around, completed a few exercises and returned to the airport for landing.

It was a very quick flight, and after another short discussion I went home. They said one of them wanted to stick to their strict employment rules about pilot's licenses but others were ready to make an exception. Now I could only wait and hope for the best. I sat in my apartment for the rest of that day thinking through every detail of that interview. *Was I good enough?* The phone rang and I saw their name come up on the caller i.d. My hand shaking, I grabbed my phone and answered.

"Good evening, Myriam. We discussed your situation further, and welcome to Conair...."

Oh my God! Time stopped. After putting my phone down, I walked in circles in my room. I thought I was dreaming. Is this really happening? Did I hear this right? No way! Oh my gosh...I did it! Not only did I get a job again, but I was going to fly an air tanker that fights fires. It was the one job I thought I would never ever be able to get. And there it was. It was actually happening. I can't even explain the feeling at that moment. The conversation replayed in my head over and over again.

"Welcome to Conair, Myriam. We were very impressed by your experiences. You are exactly what we are looking for in new candidates. Also, we could see right away that you are very comfortable flying low level and surrounded by mountains. We have no doubt that you will pass the check ride, and we will proceed as such to get your ATPL issued by Transport Canada. Ground courses start next week. Please be at the office Monday morning at eight. See you soon, and again, welcome aboard!"

And just like that, I was back in a class learning all I needed to know about this new aircraft, a Convair 580, as well as the procedures of aerial firefighting. It was a lot to take in. The company knew that we would learn most of it on the job. Of course, there was a certain standard to pass the exam and the in-flight check ride after a few weeks of training, but they were not putting too much pressure on us. And the team was incredible. The experienced guys were there to coach us, push us and motivate us all the way. I felt like I was already part of a big family. They wanted us to succeed and enjoy this incredible work we were doing. By the middle of April, I had passed my checks and got my ATPL license. I was ready for the fire season.

On the morning of April 28, I deployed with the rest of my crew. I would be based in Alberta for the season, moving from base to base depending on the fire hazard. I wouldn't return home for four months, but I was so excited about this new adventure that I knew time would fly.

Within three days, we were sent up north where a fire had started just outside of Fort McMurray. We did a few drops, and celebrated my first fire back at the base. During training we were using water, but now it was real. The splash of red from the retardant that coloured the outside of the tank was the background in the first picture with me standing beside the aircraft back on the tarmac at the end of that day. Now that was fun!

Little did I know, all hell was about to break loose.

On May 3, 2016, we were called to that same location. One fire turned into two, and suddenly it all went out of control. The fire swept through the community and forced over eighty-eight thousand people to evacuate and leave their homes and belongings behind.

I was flying every day. Many other aircraft came along to fight this wildfire, and we were all flying hours and hours non-stop trying to contain it. It took two months before it was officially declared under control. It was still smoldering all summer and wouldn't be extinguished until August. It destroyed 2,400 homes and spread over 590,000 hectares.

I was literally "baptized by fire."

My captain kept telling me this was not normal. It was all I knew so far, so I thought this was the only way things were happening. Of course, it wasn't. In a normal fire season, there would be many days of just sitting at the base doing nothing. We'd be on alert depending on the fire risks, but on stand-by, so those days can also be long and boring. Everyone found their own way to keep busy and make the long hours pass quickly. Most of the time, I would read or make puzzles, but I couldn't sit still for too long so I would walk in circles around the tarmac. I was never too far from the airplane because that bell could ring at any time. When it did, everyone dropped whatever they were doing and jumped onboard. Engines roared to life, and the tankers filled with retardant. Birddog got airborne first, followed by our tankers right behind, and we headed toward yet another wildfire.

My first season flying the Convair 580
for aerial firefighting in Canada

Looking down at one of the numerous fires raging
outside of Fort McMurray, Alberta, 2016

CONCLUSION

Looking back onto the past twenty-five years, I'm starting to believe than the Russian who called me "Sky Hunter" was right. I've definitely been chasing every corner of our sky that I could. I don't think my life will ever settle because I'm not looking for the easy path.

Three years has passed since the end of this story of mine. Many more ups and downs have kept me on my toes. As I started my third season of firefighting, health issues forced me to step down. After years of working too hard and living in less-than-healthy environments, my body decided to revoke my free pass, and it was time to take a real break to heal my body and mind. One cannot experience so much without eventually paying the price.

After too many false diagnoses and my condition worsening, I finally found someone who figured it all out and set me up with proper treatment. Within a couple of months, I could finally see some positive improvements, and a year later I was not only back on my feet, but I felt better than ever.

I could have gone back to firefighting when I was ready to return to work, though I had received an offer I could not refuse. I was going back to the Sahara to fly my favourite airplane, the Twin

CONCLUSION

Otter. This job would almost double my salary, and after being grounded for a year, I needed it. Unfortunately, this contract didn't last long, and as I was in the process of planning a new adventure, 2020 arrived.

Like so many others in the world, I am now experiencing the struggles of this global crisis. The future is uncertain, and aviation is taking a big hit for sure. Will I return to a cockpit soon? I don't know. It depends on so many factors. As I enter 2021, I am hopeful I will fly this year, but it could take much longer. Only time will tell.

In the meantime, this very strange year gave me time to slow down and reflect on what my life has been. I have learned so much through the years and grown stronger as a person after each hardship. I learned to let go what didn't really matter and hang on to what truly counts. I also realize how fulfilling my life has been; I've lived so much more than most could only dream of.

I also reconnected with my mom after my father passed. We were able to go through a healing process and talk a lot about our past. We are closer than ever and trying hard to catch up from those lost years.

Everyone spent a lot of time indoors in 2020. Nature offers me peace and happiness, and I hiked and camped more than ever. I also nurtured my passion for photography and videography. I created video mainly for my personal social media channel, but I was also asked to create a series of promotional tourism videos for the region I live in. As many have done during this wretched pandemic, being creative—like writing this book—and finding ways to keep moving forward while waiting for better times kept me busy.

My true passion for flying and living extraordinary adventures can't be replaced in any other ways. Once I tasted the adrenaline rush, I couldn't stop chasing it.

I'm not ready to stop being Sky Hunter. Not yet!

So bring on the next adventure…

ACKNOWLEDGEMENTS

For Lysle and Ron Barmby: my close friends who gave me the motivation to finally bring this project to life, as well as giving it a round of corrections.

For Mom: after too many years apart, we are now closer than ever. May this story fill in some of the gaps.

For Ulrike and Fred Leger: You read my manuscript and gave me valuable insight on my initial draft.

For my best friend whom I cannot name (you know who you are): You believed in me, trusted me and loved me. You were my mentor, my teacher and the only one who truly understood me. We wanted the impossible, we got the best and the worst, but our bond is unbreakable. You will forever have a place in my heart.

Made in the USA
Coppell, TX
19 July 2021